T0059306

YOUR
NEW
PLAYLIST

YOUR NEW PLAYLIST

THE STUDENT'S GUIDE TO TAPPING INTO
THE SUPERPOWER OF MINDSET

JON ACUFF,
WITH L.E. ACUFF
AND McRAE ACUFF

BakerBooks

a division of Baker Publishing Group
Grand Rapids, Michigan

© 2022 by Jon Acuff

Published by Baker Books
a division of Baker Publishing Group
PO Box 6287, Grand Rapids, MI 49516-6287
www.bakerbooks.com

Printed in the United States of America

Library of Congress Cataloging-in-Publication Data
Names: Acuff, Jonathan, author. | Acuff, L.E., other. | Acuff, McRae, other.
Title: Your new playlist : the student's guide to tapping into the superpower of mindset / Jon Acuff ; with L.E. Acuff, McRae Acuff.
Description: Grand Rapids, MI : Baker Books, a division of Baker Publishing Group, [2022] | Includes bibliographical references. | Audience: Ages 14–17 | Audience: Grades 10–12
Identifiers: LCCN 2022002049 | ISBN 9781540902481 (paperback) | ISBN 9781540902597 (casebound) | ISBN 9781493439324 (ebook)
Subjects: LCSH: Self-actualization (Psychology) in adolescence—Juvenile literature.
Classification: LCC BF724.3.S25 A58 2022 | DDC 155.4/19—dc23/eng/20220222
LC record available at https://lccn.loc.gov/2022002049

Published in association with Yates & Yates, www.yates2.com.

Baker Publishing Group publications use paper produced from sustainable forestry practices and post-consumer waste whenever possible.

Interior design by William Overbeeke.

23   24   25   26   27   28   7   6   5   4   3   2

From Jon:

Jenny, it takes a superhero to live
with three authors in the same house.

From L.E.:

Dad, thanks for inviting me into this fun
writing project! Also, thanks for being so tall
and funny and writing half of my dedication.

From McRae:

To the college admissions counselor reading
about this on my application: I wrote a book!

CONTENTS

Introduction

"I wish I knew then what I know now."

If you're an adult, you've said that a few times.

If you're a student, adults are jealous of you.

Why?

Because when you hit your 30s, 40s, or 50s, you learn things that would have made the school and college years so much better. Only you didn't know them then, and you don't have access to a time machine, so you're left with that sentence: "I wish I knew then what I know now."

But if you're a student, you do have access to a time machine. You're holding one in your hands right now.

Inside these pages is the fastest, funnest way to tap into the superpower of mindset.

Inside these pages are easy tools you can use to change the story you tell yourself about yourself.

Inside these pages is everything you need to create new thoughts that push you forward instead of holding you back.

I helped your parents do that when I wrote a book called *Soundtracks*. They read it, started listening to new soundtracks (my word for repetitive thoughts), and then asked me, "Will you write a version for my kid?"

The answer was, "Yes, but not alone."

I'm 46 years old. I haven't been a student for 30 years. That's a long time, and even though I've written seven other books, I knew this one had to be different. So I asked my two daughters to help me write it.

McRae is 16 years old and is a junior in high school.

L.E. (short for Laura Elizabeth and pronounced like "Ellie") is a freshman in college.

We did a collab on this project. (See, even that last sentence sounded like a dad trying to be cool.) They wrote it. I edited it. And the result is a short, powerful book that your parents wish someone had handed them when they were your age.

When you're an adult and discover that you have the power to write new soundtracks for your life, you often first have to retire broken soundtracks you've carried for years, maybe even decades.

As a student, you don't have to do that. Your life is fresh and unencumbered by the baggage we adults pick up along the way. Not only do you have less to unlearn, but you're also squarely in the learning portion of your life. From algebra to driving, students are primed to learn new things and develop new skills.

The best news is that truth tends to grow like compound interest. Saving money when you're a student has a different impact on your life than it does when you save money in your forties. A single new soundtrack believed when you're 14 or 18 can change the entire arc of your life in the same way that saving $1,000 early on can.

It's time to build some new thoughts that turn into new actions and new results.

It's time to discover how your thought life shapes your real life.

It's time to create your new playlist.

Are you ready?

Me too.

Who Turned Up
the Music?

Coach Scott:

Hey kid—unfortunately we aren't going to
be able to keep you on the team this year.
Sorry for the bad news. I truly appreciate
all the hard work you put in and your
team-first attitude. Good luck with
cross-country.

My name is McRae Acuff. I'm 16 years old,
and for two years I dreaded receiving that text.

Sometimes when your phone buzzes with a message, it's good news. A friend liked your latest post.
An artist you love released new music. A classmate

is sending the notes you missed when you were absent.

This wasn't that type of message.

I knew I might get cut from the lacrosse team, but I did everything I could to avoid it. I worked on my stamina, jogging miles through our neighborhood with my dad before our team running test. I went to lacrosse camp to work on specific skills in the off season. We bought a rebounder so I could practice throwing and catching in the backyard. I worked with friends in the neighborhood who were better than me.

I made the team as a freshman. I thought there might be a shot as a sophomore. I was wrong, and the 42 words in that text message spelled it out clearly.

It may have been a short message, and my coach was incredibly kind about it, but it caused a chain reaction of thoughts to take place within seconds:

You got cut from the team?

What a loser.

All your friends from lacrosse will never talk to you again.

Everyone at school will think you're a complete loser.

You're a loser.
Who gets cut from the team in tenth grade?
All of your friends are still on the team except you.
You were the worst on the team, so it makes sense you got cut.

Before I could even tell my parents what just happened, a thousand thoughts flooded my head. I felt emotionally overwhelmed and out of control—lost in the flow of negativity. In that moment, I found myself asking a question I've asked hundreds of times:

Who turned up the music so loud?

Sometimes it feels like my thoughts are crashing a party I don't remember inviting any of them to.

My geometry test has parked a car right in the middle of my front yard.

Homecoming is banging pots and pans in the kitchen.

Tryouts for the school play are jumping up and down on my bed so hard that the ceiling is shaking.

I'm trying to do homework. I'm trying to eat dinner with my family. I'm trying to get ready for school. I'm trying to do anything but think about those thoughts, but those thoughts are loud.

Have your thoughts ever felt that way too? Like

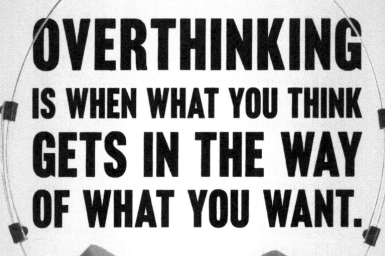

OVERTHINKING IS WHEN WHAT YOU THINK GETS IN THE WAY OF WHAT YOU WANT.

JON ACUFF

#YourNewPlaylist

the music you're listening to got stuck and you can't change songs? It's like Spotify Rewind, when they send you your most played songs of the year and the list only has a handful:

1. The ACT is coming up and you're not ready.
2. You didn't get invited to that party that's on all your friends' stories.
3. There's not a good spot to sit at lunch.

Your thoughts might have different words than mine, but every student does this exact same thing sometimes. It's called *overthinking*, and it's when what you think gets in the way of what you want.

You want to enjoy the football game without overthinking why your friend didn't respond to your text yet.

You want to apply to college without overthinking that you should have done more extracurricular activities when you were a freshman.

You want to get your driver's license without overthinking how uncool you look behind the wheel of your mom's minivan.

But overthinking gets in the way.

If you've ever worried that you're the only one who does that, I've got some good news: you're not.

A researcher named Mike Peasley, who has a PhD, recently asked more than 10,000 people if they struggle with overthinking, and more than 99.5 percent of them answered yes.

Isn't that crazy? When I say everyone does it, I mean EVERYONE.

It's not a personality trait. It's not because you did something wrong. It's not because you're weird. Overthinking is something that happens to all of us and causes a lot of trouble.

Overthinking steals your dreams, cripples your confidence, and tangles you up when you least expect it.

But what if it didn't have to?

What if your thoughts could work for you, not against you?

What if you could create a new playlist?

What if—and this next part is going to sound a little too good to be true—you could tap into the superpower of mindset?

You can, and that's what this book is all about.

Though this is my first book, it's my dad's eighth book. His last one was called *Soundtracks: The Surprising Solution to*—you guessed it—*Overthinking*. When it came time to write a version of it for students, he asked me and my sister L.E. to help.

Although he occasionally will say popular phrases

like "dope" or "no cap" (usually years after they've gone out of style), he's not a teenager. He hasn't been a teenager since 1994, and a lot has changed since then. Smartphones didn't exist. The internet didn't exist. Social media didn't exist. Netflix didn't exist. The music of the 80s might have been great, but my dad grew up in a very different world from you and me.

It's easier than ever for you and me to overthink.

So instead of trying to pretend he understood what it meant to be a student in today's world, he gave us the chance to talk with you. L.E. and I are going to tag team the chapters ahead and will say our names when there's a specific story one of us is telling.

This is bigger than just our story though. There are hundreds of students represented in these pages. My dad is a public speaker. Companies, colleges, and camps hire him to speak. Ten years ago, at high school presentations, he started teaching students about the power of mindset. At the end of his speeches, he'd ask them to write down the stories they were telling themselves about themselves. Each student would drop off what they anonymously wrote on pieces of paper in boxes at the back of the room.

It was an exercise that gave them a chance to get

something off their chests as well as an opportunity to have their voices heard. We still have boxes of those personal soundtracks in our house. Between those notes and DMs and conversations with friends in the cafeteria, when we started writing about the superpower of mindset, the floodgate of student thoughts opened up.

It turns out L.E. and I aren't the only students who could use a new playlist.

Whether you're a 15-year-old boy in Oklahoma, a 19-year-old girl in Florida, or somewhere in between, you'll be able to see yourself inside this book.

More than likely a parent gave you this. Hopefully there was a $20 bill slid into the back page as a reward for finishing it. Tell them I said that's part of the official reading plan, because who doesn't want a free $20?

Inside, we're going to teach you how to do three things:

1. Retire your broken soundtracks.

2. Replace them with new soundtracks.

3. Repeat the new ones so often that they become as automatic as the old ones.

Retire, replace, and repeat.

That's it.

If it sounds simple, that's because it is.

Getting cut from the lacrosse team wasn't easy, but knowing how to deal with my soundtracks changed my mindset in that moment, which changed how I responded and ultimately changed what happened next. (Spoiler alert: The story ends well!)

Tapping into the superpower of mindset can do the same for you.

All it takes is a new playlist.

Let's start building yours.

The Wrong Songs

She didn't shout when she climbed out of the pool, but her words still hit her mom like a lightning bolt.

I (L.E.) wasn't trying to listen in on what was clearly a private conversation, but there's never a lot of room when you're lining up for your heat at a swim meet. It's always an awkward collection of wet kids jammed together under pop-up tents.

I was on the swim team when I was in high school, and my summer days were often spent on the side of a pool waiting for my race to start. I didn't know the swimmer who brushed by me that day, but it was impossible to miss what she said.

Covered in chlorine and disappointment, she locked eyes briefly with her mom and then proclaimed to no one and everyone, "I suck at swimming. I'm the slowest swimmer ever. I'm the worst person on the team." Then she trudged away to reluctantly get ready for her next race.

Her mother was speechless, perhaps all too familiar with statements like this. But I couldn't help having my own opposite reaction to the scene. "Those are just broken soundtracks. She can change that," I thought to myself.

That idea quickly jumped into my head because for years my dad and my little sister McRae have talked about exactly that. It can always be a little awkward when you change narrators in a book, so I'll keep this brief. My name is L.E., I'm 19 years old, and I attend Samford University in Birmingham, Alabama.

Some people describe thoughts as leaves on a river, clouds in the sky, or cars on the highway, but at our house we always call them soundtracks. That word is a fun way to think about your thoughts because a soundtrack is one of those things that often plays in the background. You might not even notice it, but it has the power to change the entire moment.

Think about what music does to a simple TikTok video. At the time we were writing this, one popular meme involved placing a misquoted line from a Sam Smith song that says "By the way, she's safe with me" onto a video of your boyfriend, girlfriend, or even your dog. It was meant to change a simple clip of someone walking down the beach into a statement piece essentially saying, "You hurt this person in the past, but now she's safe with me." A single lyric changes the mood from a casual video into a complex, emotionally charged, baggage-heavy scene about rescue and redemption. That's just one example. It feels like half of going viral on TikTok is finding the right song or sound.

Soundtracks change EVERYTHING, and that's how your thoughts work too.

The loudest thoughts you have—the ones you might have listened to for years—never just stay thoughts. They always turn into actions, and those actions turn into results.

If you tell yourself a thousand times that you won't make the soccer team, guess what happens? You don't try out for the soccer team. If you don't try out, guess what result you get? You don't make the soccer team. Your thought turned into an action that turned into a result.

This isn't something that happens only to high school students. Scientists have been studying it for years. The craziest example happened at New York University. Researchers there did a study to see how powerful thoughts can be. They brought two groups of college students into a room and asked them to make sentences out of a word bank, which is just a random collection of words on a piece of paper.[1]

Both groups made as many sentences as they could, but there was something slightly different about the words the second group of students was given. Hidden in that word bank were ideas related to old age. Words such as *bald*, *Florida*, and *wrinkle* were sprinkled throughout their set. You know your state is full of old people when it's used as an example in a scientific study!

At the end of the word challenge, the scientists told the students to walk down the hall to complete the second portion of the study in another classroom. As they made their way down the hall, the real test began. The scientists secretly timed the students to see how long it took them to make the short trip. The students exposed to the set of old-age words walked slower.

Just reading the words about being elderly caused a physical change!

That's wild, but it makes sense when you think about it. A friend who says something mean to you first thing in the morning can ruin your whole day as you replay that conversation in your head. An exam you're dreading on Monday can reshape your whole weekend. A date you're looking forward to can make your entire week feel bright and hopeful.

Your thoughts are the internal soundtracks you listen to, and they impact every part of your life. The longer you listen to a certain thought, the more it becomes part of your personal playlist.

That wasn't the first time the frustrated swimmer had thought, "I'm the slowest swimmer on the team." It was probably the thousandth time. She had listened to that soundtrack so often that if she was off her race time by even a fraction of a second, it would play automatically.

That's how our brains work. The fancy term is *cognitive bias*, but it basically means that your brain likes to believe what it already believes. It's biased to believe old soundtracks. So if you believe you're a slow swimmer, it will look for proof of that. It will collect evidence to back that up, like a lawyer preparing for a court case against you. Your brain is kind of a jerk that way.

Your soundtracks playing automatically wouldn't be such a bad thing though—if they were positive. Who wouldn't want positive thoughts playing in their head all day?

"You're going to make the football team!"

"People like you!"

"You get invited to all the fun parties!"

"You got this!"

"You're definitely capable of passing that class!"

"It's OK that you don't have it all figured out. Nobody does at your age!"

That would be amazing, but raise your hand if that's what all your soundtracks sound like. Most of mine certainly don't, and you and I aren't the only ones. I know firsthand how negative soundtracks sound because I've read through hundreds of them in those boxes of anonymous notes from students that McRae mentioned in the last chapter.

I wish I could say they were encouraging like the ones I listed above, but that would be a lie. Instead, they said things like this:

"None of your friends really like you. They're just being nice."

"You're not skinny enough, despite how much you work out."

"You're worthless."

"You will fail your future family because your parents failed theirs."

"Don't break up with him, because no one else wants you."

"Your troubles with your mom are all your fault."

Those are broken soundtracks, repetitive thoughts that make life harder, not easier. But how do you know if you have one? If the first step to tapping into the superpower of mindset is to retire your broken soundtracks, how do you even identify one?

It's a lot easier than you think. In fact, all it takes is a 30-second exercise. I'll teach you exactly how to do it in the next chapter.

How to Spot a Broken Soundtrack

Maybe you read through the list of examples in the last chapter and had a really easy time identifying a broken soundtrack that's holding you back. Maybe you're a swimmer too, and that was the most specific story you've ever read in a book. But maybe you're not even sure if you have a broken soundtrack. That's OK, because there's a simple way to find them, and it only has two steps.

Step 1: Write down a goal.

That's all I (L.E.) want you to do. Write down a goal. Write down a dream. Write down a wish.

It can be anything. It could be big, like "I want to

get into Princeton" or "I wish my parents would get back together." It could be small, like "I want to visit the beach this summer" or "I want to get a dog." It could be somewhere in between, like "I want to have a friend I can trust." Write down anything you'd like to be true in your life.

That's the first step, and feel free to be as honest as you want to. This isn't homework. You don't have to submit this in Google Classroom or turn this in to a professor. You won't be graded. There's no way to fail this assignment. You're the only one who will see this. So, even if your goal is so big it feels ridiculous to say it out loud, do it anyway.

Step 2: Listen to the first thoughts you have.

What were the very first thoughts you heard when you wrote down that goal?

Were they encouraging? Maybe you heard something like "You should do that! You'd be great at doing that. You're the best age to do something like that. People are going to support that goal."

Or were your soundtracks just the opposite? Maybe they sounded like, "Who are you to do that? You could never do that. You're too young. That will never work."

Listen to your reaction, because every reaction is

an education. Your reaction is trying to teach you about the way you think.

If your reaction is positive, that's great. You've got the kind of soundtracks everyone wants to listen to. You should listen to those as often as you can because they're so encouraging.

If your reaction is negative, that's great too, because now you've got something to work with. Changing the story you tell yourself about yourself is a process.

You don't have to do it all at once. You don't have to do it overnight. You don't even have to deal with all your thoughts. You have thousands of thoughts every day! Who has time to work through all of that? I don't. So instead, we're going to keep it simple.

All we're going to do is ask our loudest soundtracks three questions so that we can retire them.

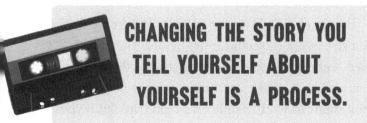

CHANGING THE STORY YOU TELL YOURSELF ABOUT YOURSELF IS A PROCESS.

The Three Magic Questions

Who do you think is the second-best character in
the Harry Potter books?

The best character is obviously Luna Lovegood.
I (McRae) know she's the best character because, in
addition to being brave, artsy, and fully comfortable
in her own skin, there are four dogs in my neighborhood named Luna. But I think you could definitely
debate who is the silver medalist of Hogwarts.

I haven't met a single dog named Snape.

I haven't met a cat named Hagrid.

I haven't even met a hamster named Albus
Dumbledore, which is a hilariously large name for
such a small pet. But I've met some Lunas. Our
neighborhood is crawling with them. I love seeing
them on walks because it always reminds me of how
much I enjoy those books.

I don't believe in magic, but I do believe the three
questions I'm going to teach you are about as close
as we Muggles can get.

They're so simple on the outside. They're words
you've heard a thousand times before. They won't
even seem special the first time you see them. They'd
never make it onto a vocabulary quiz or help you
look smart to your friends on a road trip. But if you
sit with them for a minute and use them in the right

order, you're going to feel like you just might have a lightning bolt scar on your forehead.

Did you write down any broken soundtracks from the last chapter? If not, that's OK. Reading a book your parents probably gave you AND writing down notes in it is a pretty big ask. Maybe see if they can bump up that $20 bill in the back to $50. You might end up with $100 at the end of the day if you play your cards right.

You don't have to take notes unless you want to, but the next time you hear a broken soundtrack, the next time you tell yourself something that's discouraging, negative, or maybe even mean, I want you to ask the first question.

QUESTION 1:
Is It True?

Is the story you're telling yourself about yourself—about a situation, about a friend, about anything—true?

One of the greatest mistakes you can make is assuming that all your thoughts are true. Despite the lies our thoughts have told us over and over again, we tend to believe that if we think something, it must be true. If it's in our head, it must be fact. But what if it's not?

When my dad was in middle school, his answer to the question "What's your goal?" would have been, "To own a BB gun." It's not the biggest aspiration. I mean, "world peace" sounds a lot better on a college application. But that was his big wish.

ONE OF THE GREATEST MISTAKES YOU CAN MAKE IS ASSUMING THAT ALL YOUR THOUGHTS ARE TRUE.

Every time he imagined that BB gun, he heard a few soundtracks.

Your parents will never let you own a BB gun.

Your parents will kill you if you buy a BB gun.

Your parents don't want you to own a BB gun because they are trying to ruin your life.

That last one is a bit comical, but let's be honest: we've all thought it at some point. We've all bumped into some rule or regulation our parents came up with that felt life-ending.

Did you get your first phone as early as you wanted to? I (McRae) know I didn't. I feel like my parents made me wait forever. Same with Instagram. My parents gave that to my older sister as a Christmas present one year. That's right, my parents printed out the Instagram logo, wrapped it, and then gave it to her. It's a free app, but they wanted her to know it came with some expectations.

My dad was convinced his parents wouldn't let him own a BB gun, but he never stopped for a second to ask, "Is it true?"

If he had, I know they would have bought him one. It would have come with some rules, of course, but my grandfather is the kind of person who loves giving kids fun gifts. Last Christmas he gave my dad an industrial-strength laser pointer that's so strong you can practically hit the moon with it. I bet if I asked him for a set of throwing axes for my birthday he would oblige. He's a fun, silly, build-a-fort-in-the-woods-with-you kind of grandfather. He might have taken a little bit of convincing, but I'm sure he would have joined TeamBBGun.

But my dad listened to all those broken soundtracks and convinced himself that his parents were against him. Unfortunately, as we learned in chapter 2, thoughts usually don't just stay thoughts. They tend to become actions that eventually become results.

My dad turned the thought "Your parents will never let you own a BB gun" into an action. He secretly bought a BB gun from a friend who was moving to Colorado.

He didn't have his driver's license at the time, so he lied to his mom and said, "Would you please drive me to Brad Dale's house so that I can say good-bye to him one last time?"

He was really tugging on the heartstrings, wasn't he?

His mom fell for it, and when she also went inside the Dales' house to say goodbye to the family, my dad ran out the back door while she was distracted. He hid the gun and a box of BBs in the back of their minivan. The whole ride home he had to talk extra loud so his mom wouldn't hear the BBs rolling around in the box.

As a new BB gun owner, he decided that the next best step was to set up a shooting range in his bed-room. Yes, you read that correctly: my dad set up a shooting range in his bedroom. It wasn't a 100-foot bedroom either. It wasn't long and skinny like a weird pencil-shaped bedroom, if that's what you're thinking. It was a 10-foot-square room that they built in a garage smaller than any classroom you sit in.

Do you know what happens when you shoot Coke cans with a BB gun in your room? The BBs go right through the can and lodge into your wall. Do you know what happens when you do that a dozen times? Your mom eventually notices the collection of BBs stuck in your wall and you get grounded.

All he had to do before the whole misadventure

started was ask, "Is it true?" when his soundtracks told him, "Your parents are out to ruin your life." Instead he came up with an elaborate plan that ended in a whole host of lies, a makeshift indoor shooting range, and punishment.

Maybe you won't try that exact thing, but today or tomorrow you're going to bump into a loud soundtrack. When you do, ask that first question:

Is it true?

One easy way to know it's not true is if you hear absolutes in the soundtrack. For example:

"I'll *never* learn algebra."

"*Everyone* has a phone except me."

"I'll *always* feel lonely."

"I'm the slowest swimmer on the *entire* team."

"I'm the *only* one who won't get into college."

Words like *never*, *everyone*, *always*, *entire*, and *only* are usually not true. It might take you a year or maybe even two, but eventually you'll learn algebra. You're not the only one who doesn't have a phone. Someone else at your school doesn't have one, and they might not even have Instagram or Snapchat because it isn't Christmas yet!

Feelings change every day, sometimes by the hour.

You won't always feel lonely. You and I won't always
be any one thing, because we're constantly changing.
Don't let absolute soundtracks like *always* and *never*
sneak into your life. They tend to be absolute lies.

"Is it true?" is the first question you should always
ask a broken soundtrack.

QUESTION 2:

Is It Helpful?

The question "Is it true?" isn't enough to expose the lie in a broken soundtrack. That's why it's so frustrating when someone says, "Stop overthinking that situation—it isn't true!"

You might know logically that you're not the only guy who doesn't own an Xbox or that your entire life won't fall apart if all your friends make varsity and you're stuck on JV, but both of those things *feel* true in the moment. That's why we need to ask a second question:

Is it helpful?

Is the soundtrack you have on repeat right now helpful? When you listen to it, do you feel

encouraged or discouraged? Do you feel energized
or drained? Does it inspire you to make good decisions or bad decisions?

"Is it helpful?" is a pretty easy question you can
apply to almost every area of your life. Sometimes
I (McRae) take breaks from Instagram. I don't always walk away from Instagram feeling excited
about my life. There are just some weeks I get stuck
scrolling endlessly, and when I'm done I don't feel
encouraged.

Spring break can be one of those weeks. It's easy
to see a parade of photos from friends on beach trips
you weren't invited to and feel left out. Is it helpful for me to spend hours on Instagram feeling that
way? Usually the answer is no, so I put it aside for a
week or two.

It's also good to have a second magic question
because there are some soundtracks that are true but
not helpful. For instance, I once got a 42 on a biology test. That is true.

The soundtrack "I got a 42 on my biology test" is
a fact. That's a thing that 100 percent did happen.
And in case you're wondering—yes, that was with
the curve.

That soundtrack is true, but does listening to it
over and over again help me? Is reminding myself of
that for weeks helpful?

It's not, especially when I'm studying for the next exam. The problem is that soundtracks tend to grow negative over time if you don't work on them.

It's easy for "I got a 42 on my biology test" to turn into "I got a 42 on my biology test and that might happen again." Then, if I listen to that one a few times, it could turn into "I got a 42 on my biology test and I'll never pass this class." Uh-oh. Do you see what just happened? *Never* made an appearance in my soundtrack like a bonus scene at the end of a Marvel movie.

If, while studying for my next test, I tell myself, "I'll never pass this class. I'll never pass this class. I'll never pass this class," do you think that's helpful?

Of course not. What a terrible soundtrack to listen to while you're studying for a test.

This second question will even change who I talk with before a test. We all have friends who add drama to situations. (I know you're thinking of someone specific right now!) These are the friends who talk about how much they're dreading a test, how hard they heard it was going to be, how difficult the teacher is, and on and on. If I spend 15 minutes on the bus rehearsing that drama with friends, is it helpful?

It's not. So, when I have a big exam, I do my best

to avoid conversations with friends who are going to throw fuel on the fire right before I take it.

As soon as you start asking this second question, you're going to be surprised to discover how many situations you're putting yourself in that aren't helpful.

Start with "Is it true?" Then ask "Is it helpful?" And then move on to what I think is the easiest of the three questions.

QUESTION 3:
Is It Kind?

All three of these questions are simple, but this one might be the simplest:

Is it kind?

Is the soundtrack you're listening to kind to yourself?

Another way to say it is, "If you said this to a friend, would they still want to be your friend?" That's an easy one to answer yes or no to, right?

If I (McRae) texted my friend 100 times in one night saying, "You'll never pass this class, you'll never pass this class, you'll never pass this class," would she still want to be my friend? Nope. Who wants friends like that?

So, if you wouldn't say it to a friend, why are you saying it to yourself? Why is the meanest person we've ever met often ourselves?

Maybe it's because there are so many expectations on students these days with social media. For example, do you know how your mom got asked to prom? A boy came up to her and said, "Do you want to go to prom?" That was the whole experience, and no one took a picture of her response. No one captured it from multiple angles. No one posted it on their story. No one compared how that boy asked her to how other boys asked other girls, because they all did the same thing.

Back then there were no promposals. Now, though, if someone doesn't ask you with a funny sign, beautiful balloons, and a helicopter that drops flowers from the sky, you feel "less than." Social media has skyrocketed our expectations of how life should be, and when we don't measure up, we beat ourselves up.

That's unfortunate, because now we're in a constant fight with the person we spend the most time with: ourselves. Have you ever thought about that? You spend more time with you than anyone else. And if you're not kind to you, it's like hanging out with a jerk all day.

That's why your soundtracks matter. The story you

IF YOU'RE NOT **KIND** TO YOU, IT'S LIKE HANGING OUT WITH A JERK ALL DAY.

JON ACUFF

#YourNewPlaylist

tell yourself about yourself is the story you'll hear
more than any other in your entire life. Even more
than Harry Potter.

Is it true?

Is it helpful?

Is it kind?

Those are the three questions you should ask your
loudest soundtracks. If you can't answer yes to all of
them, then it's time to retire that broken soundtrack.

To do that, we're going to learn about the power
of the dial.

The Dial and the Switch

What do you talk about the most in your house?

Maybe it's a sports team your family is crazy about.

Maybe it's your dog who takes center stage of most conversations.

Maybe it's a younger sister who's just learning to walk or an older brother who is about to get married.

Every family has a handful of things they focus on the most. One year for me (L.E.) it was the show *Stranger Things*. I was obsessed. I had posters on my wall, kept a massive playlist of all the 1980s songs from the episodes, and even paid hundreds of dollars to meet one of the characters. That's right, I spent a year saving up so that I could get a photo with Millie Bobby Brown, who plays Eleven, at a Sheraton by the airport.

One year all my friend Garrett talked about with his family was girls he wanted to date. Whether it was homecoming, winter formal, Valentine's Day, or Flag Day, he took any chance he could to ask a girl out. He had a new job at a golf course, a new driver's license, and a new hope that there was a serious girlfriend out there for him. His house could have been on fire and he would've told you about a potential friendzone disaster he was trying to avoid in precalculus class.

When I was in high school, there was a group of students who constantly talked about lettuce. They started a lettuce club, where the only goal was to be the person who could eat a head of lettuce fastest at each meeting. I'm not sure that's good for you, but it certainly made for interesting flyers hung up in the cafeteria.

From favorite TV shows to dating relationships and apparently even lettuce, we all have topics of conversation that keep coming up. One that pops up regularly for the Acuffs is the difference between a dial and a switch.

If that sounds a little weird, you're right. When your dad is an author, you tend to have unusual conversations at the dinner table. As soon as you read this idea, though, you're going to be talking about it at your house too.

It's Not a Switch

David Thomas is cooler than my dad. My dad is going to edit this whole book, so who knows if that sentence will make the final cut, but he knows it's true.

David is the kind of dad who can wear Air Jordans and not look like he's a dad trying to wear Air Jordans. He's also the author of six books, an accomplished public speaker, and the director of family counseling at Daystar, a center for kids in Nashville.

When you're in college like me, you start to get curious about what's next. You start to wonder, "Who has the kind of life I'd like to have someday?" You might not be ready for a mentor, but you do start to pay attention to adults who seem to be having fun in the hope that you could have fun at that age too. David is like that.

One of the ideas he teaches students like us is that there's a big difference between a dial and a switch. He says, "The problem with the internal voices we hear is that we want a switch. We think that there's a switch out there and if we can just find it, we can turn off the background noise completely. We only have to do it one time and we'll never hear it again. People want there to be a switch."[1]

Have you ever felt that way?

Have you ever felt like maybe if you just got the right grade in a class, got into THE college, dated the right person, or got a certain number of Instagram followers, all your negative voices would stop bothering you? Maybe for you it was a phone. You had the oldest phone in your friend circle, or maybe you didn't even have one. You told yourself, "As soon as I get a new phone, I won't feel this way anymore."

What always happens though?

The post you hoped would get 100 likes got 100 likes, and that felt good for a minute, but 200 likes would be even better. And there's another photo you'll post tomorrow that starts the counter all over again. The stress might calm down for a minute, but it always comes back. No matter which switch we turn off, somehow it's never enough.

David Thomas says the reason is simple:

> It's not a switch, it's a dial. The goal isn't to turn it off forever, the goal is to turn down the volume. It's going to get louder sometimes. That's how dials work. But when life turns up the negative thoughts,

we get to turn them down. That takes a lot of the pressure off because when you hear a negative thought again, it's not a sign that you've failed to shut it off and need to go find a different switch. It's just time for an action that will turn it back down.[2]

What if that's why so many of us feel such pressure? We thought there was a switch. We thought everyone else had access to it. We thought it would fix everything, so we started searching for it. At home, at school, at the mall, on the football field, at work, in the cafeteria, online—we looked everywhere for the switch but just couldn't seem to locate it.

The annoying thing is that companies know this. Can you guess why you suddenly hate your current phone and want the next one? Because someone wearing a suit at a big meeting in an office said, "How do we get students to hate their current phones and want the next one?"

Life is hard enough without entire companies spending billions of dollars on advertising to try and get us to believe their product is the switch that will fix everything. But what if life is a dial, not a switch? What if instead of searching for a solution out there, we already have what we need right here?

If you have soundtracks that aren't true, helpful,

or kind, that's not a big deal. It just means your dial got turned up.

And guess what you get to do in response? Turn it down. That's one of the best ways to tap into the superpower of mindset.

Dials Always Go Two Directions

I (L.E.) **don't know about you,** but sometimes life feels overwhelming when you're a student. Balancing classes, sports, extracurricular activities, relationships, jobs, college applications, and a thousand other things feels complicated. But dials aren't that way at all. Dials are actually incredibly simple. They only have two directions.

Everything in life does one of two things to you:

1. It turns your dial up.
2. It turns your dial down.

Things that turn your dial up make you stressed out. They make you feel frustrated, upset, sad, scared, or confused.

Things that turn your dial down do just the opposite. They calm you down. They add peace to your life. They make you feel confident, happy, safe, and content.

Think about the last time you felt stuck or disappointed. Read through this list and see if any of these things had happened:

1. You had an argument with your parents.
2. You made a bad grade on an exam and started to believe you'd never get into college because of one rough test.
3. You saw photos online for a party you didn't get invited to.
4. You didn't know who to talk to at the football game and ended up sitting with your parents instead of in the student section.
5. Tryouts for your favorite team were coming up.
6. Someone who doesn't work as hard as you got a better grade on an assignment.
7. You don't have anyone to go to homecoming with.

8. You can't afford to go on an expensive spring break like your friends.
9. It's Friday night and you don't have anything to do.
10. Your boss keeps leaving you off the schedule at work.
11. You don't know what you want to study in college.
12. You found out a friend has been gossiping about you.
13. You didn't get the part you wanted in the school play.
14. You feel like you're the only person your age who doesn't have a car.
15. Every teacher decided to assign something massive at the same exact time.

Maybe even reading through that list made you feel a little queasy. The problem is that when things like that happen to us, we usually don't pause and say, "Wait a second, what's really going on right now? What just turned up my dial?"

Instead, we beat ourselves up. We think, "What's wrong with me? Why am I this way? I shouldn't feel this way. I'm the only one who feels like this." And we then put our broken soundtracks on repeat, listening to them for hours, maybe even weeks.

It doesn't have to be that way though. What if the next time you felt stressed, you said out loud, "My dial is really high right now. I'm at a 10 out of 10. I wonder why?"

More than likely you'd be able to identify the culprit quickly. Even if you just scanned through the three Fs—*family*, *friends*, and *future*—I bet one would stand out.

Family

Is there tension between me and my parents? Am I not getting along with my brother? Am I tired of sharing a bedroom with my little sister? Do I feel like my older sibling gets all the attention? Do I feel pressure to live up to my mom's expectations? Are my parents divorced and I'm tired of shuffling between their two houses? Maybe there's a family situation that has raised your dial.

Friends

Is my friend group changing? Now that we've all moved on to high school or college, does it feel like we're splitting apart? Do I feel out of the loop because most of my friends play a sport I don't play and it's all they talk about? Does it feel like all my friends are in relationships but me? Was I hoping to have a date to prom by now? Maybe there's a friends situation that raised your dial.

Future

Am I concerned about a grade? Is paying for college something that's gotten loud in my mind lately? Do I feel trapped in this small town where I live? Am I overthinking ways to make my senior year perfect so I don't regret anything? Everyone else is a cheerleader or a drama kid or a history major, but I don't know what my real passion is. Am I worried that I don't know what my "thing" is yet? Maybe there's a future situation that has raised your dial.

Maybe it's not any of those three things. But what if you could pause the next time your dial is turned up and fill out this simple statement:

"When I [insert action], I feel [insert emotion]."

When I spend hours on social media looking at everyone else's life, I feel inadequate about my own.

When I drink with friends, I feel ashamed later.

When I spend time with my friend Clarissa, I feel exhausted after.

When I talk with people before a big test, I feel more stressed out about it.

When I make my bedroom messy, I feel cluttered inside too.

The goal of doing an exercise like this is to build a little self-awareness.

Think about self-awareness like knowing what kind of car you are. A Ferrari would be terrible at off-roading. It's only about six inches off the ground and would get stuck constantly. A Jeep would lose every street race it was in. It's slow and heavy, with tires designed for trails, not the track. But no one takes a Ferrari into the mud or a Jeep into a race, because we know how they work best.

That's what self-awareness is: learning how you work best.

SELF-AWARENESS IS LEARNING HOW YOU WORK BEST.

The more you know about who you are, the easier it is to win at life. So, the first question to think about is, "What turns my dial up?"

I gave you 15 examples above, but I bet you can think of your own too.

The second and, in my opinion, much more fun question is the one in the next chapter: "What turns my dial down?"

Let's explore that one right now.

Turn-Down Techniques

This is McRae! I had to jump in because this is my favorite chapter in the book and I have a turn-down technique you're going to love. What's a turn-down technique? It's something you do whenever you realize your dial is turned up. It's a simple activity that helps you take the volume down to a more manageable level.

Here's a list of 15 examples:

1. Making a list of things you are grateful for.
2. Going for a walk outside by yourself.
3. Taking a few deep breaths.
4. Driving to some of your favorite, upbeat music.
5. Playing with your dog or cat. (I assume there

are people reading this whose fathers love them enough to buy them a dog—hint, hint.)

6. Reading a book you can get lost in.

7. Cleaning your room or organizing your closet.

8. Playing your favorite sport. It's hard to be stressed when you're exhausted from soccer practice.

9. Ranting in your journal or notes app.

10. Hanging out with your best friend.

11. Taking a break from social media. (This one is going to come up a lot because it feels like social media is a broken soundtrack factory!)

12. Reading positive affirmations or encouraging statements.

13. Eating your favorite snack.

14. Talking to someone older who you trust.

15. Playing a few songs you like on an instrument.

Some of those probably sound terrible to you. Some of them probably sound awesome. That last one is torture for me. I can't play an instrument to save my life. L.E., on the other hand, loves to play the piano as a turn-down technique. Maybe #7, cleaning your room, is the last thing you want to do. The key is that the technique has to be personal to you. For example, some people hate running. I like to run, though, so when I notice my dial is at a 9 out of 10, I head out to jog a mile.

Who am I kidding? My dial goes way higher than 10. My dial goes up to 100! There are a lot of little notches on it. Every student's dial is different. I have friends who never seem to get as stressed as I do. It's like their dial only goes to 5. Sometimes I get a little jealous, but then I remember that everyone is different. Some people love the pressure of being a goalie in hockey or soccer, but I would never want to play that position.

When life gets loud—and it's going to—you don't give up or stay stuck. You get out your list of turn-down techniques and see which one would help the most in that moment. (It's usually more than one!)

While working on this book, I realized that I have five general turn-down techniques I use. I was having a hard time remembering them, so I turned them into an acronym. I blame the ACT, PSAT, and SAT for teaching me to think in acronyms.

Here's what I use: JEEPS.

J is for Jesus

Faith is an important part of my life. When I feel stressed, an encouraging worship song, a simple prayer, or a Bible verse really helps me.

E is for Eat

Sometimes my stress is just because I'm hungry. The Snickers commercial that says "You're not you when you're hungry" is true! If I haven't eaten all day and my blood sugar is in the dumps, it's easy for me to get discouraged. The same thing happens if I've been eating a ton of junk. The dial gets turned up and I don't feel great physically or emotionally. A good meal often helps me turn it down.

E is for Exercise

Endorphins are my best friend, but that's only because my parents refuse to buy me a dog. A short walk around the neighborhood can really lift my spirits when some broken soundtrack gets loud. If I notice the dial is high, I can often easily trace it back to the fact that I haven't exercised in weeks.

P is for People

I need community. Even when I'm feeling introverted, a good friend can really encourage me. If I hide out in my room all weekend binge-watching TV or scrolling on my phone, I can tell an immediate difference. Isolation cranks that dial up! In moments like these, I do my best to reach out to people.

S is for Sleep

I suck without sleep. It's true. If I don't get sleep, I'm a mess. Nothing about life feels easier when I'm exhausted. I used to fight naps when I was a kid, but now I see the benefit of them. Getting to bed on time tends to naturally turn my dial down the next day.

When I feel stressed, it's easy to take out my little notecard that has JEEPS written on it and check in. Usually what I find is that it's been days since I've slept enough or weeks since I've reached out to friends. The S and the P are missing.

Once I realize that, it's a little easier for me to jump back in to what I know has worked in the past and what I know will work in the future too. I might not feel like it at first, but walking around the neighborhood will make me feel better after.

That's one of the soundtracks we say in our family: "I'll feel awesome after." There are so many things that might feel inconvenient, dumb, or maybe even scary at first but that feel awesome after. I might feel like I'm bothering a friend if I reach out and ask them to throw the Frisbee with me, but after we've talked and I've had a little bit of community, I always feel better.

I wish I could tell you something that would completely remove all the stress from your life forever. I wish I had a trick or a technique that would make high school, college, and adulthood worry-free, but I don't. There are going to be some challenging moments in college. There are going to be some stressful moments when you're 25 or 35 or, if my great-grandfather is any indication, even when you're 91! But when they happen, you'll know what to do.

The next time a broken soundtrack gets loud, retire it with a turn-down technique.

I shared 15 examples of techniques that work for me and my friends, but you don't have to use those. Come up with your own. If dressing your cat up like Katniss Everdeen, putting it in a baby stroller, and walking it around the neighborhood while listening to the theme song from *The Office* turns your dial down, go for it. It's your life. Your turn-down techniques don't need to work for anyone else but you.

Once you have a few, you'll be ready for what I think is the best part of tapping into the superpower of mindset: replacing your broken soundtracks with music you actually want to hear.

10

All Your Favorite Songs

Did anyone ever teach you how to think?

Did you ever have a class at school called "How to Select the Thoughts You Want to Have Today"?

Did anyone ever help you pick out your thoughts before a big test, audition, or tryout?

Probably not. Most people, including the adults in your life, don't know that they can choose what they think. Instead, what did you hear while growing up? Maybe you heard things like,

"Stop overthinking it!"

"It's all in your head."

"It's not a big deal."

Those statements are as common as dads in white New Balances. Every student has heard them.

The first one is impossible. You're a thinking

MOST PEOPLE,
INCLUDING THE ADULTS IN YOUR LIFE,
DON'T KNOW THAT THEY CAN

CHOOSE
WHAT THEY
THINK.

JON ACUFF

#YourNewPlaylist

machine. You were designed to think thousands and thousands of thoughts every day. You couldn't stop thinking if you wanted to.

The second statement isn't helpful, and the last one isn't true. It *is* a big deal, even if what you're going through doesn't look like a big deal to anyone else. That's just how your brain works. It has a hard time distinguishing real trauma from fake trauma. Let me (L.E.) explain what I mean.

Researchers at the University of Michigan Medical School found that when we experience a social rejection, our brains release the same kind of opioids they release during a physical trauma. Even when the participants in a scientific study knew ahead of time that the social rejection was fake and part of an experiment, the result was the same. Our brains hit the panic button and dump opioids into our bodies to help us survive the perceived emotional pain.[1]

I felt like a chemistry teacher there for a minute, so let me say it more simply:

When faced with fake rejection, your body releases real chemicals.

Your boyfriend dumping you in high school might not seem like a big deal in the grand scheme of things, but tell that to your brain. When that happens or when a friend unadds you on Snapchat or a thousand of the other challenges we face as students,

WHEN FACED WITH FAKE REJECTION, YOUR BODY RELEASES REAL CHEMICALS.

our brains light up. They shout, "Danger! Danger! Danger!" and then we overreact in some way that only causes more drama.

Why does this happen? Because as we learned earlier, our thoughts become our actions and our actions become results.

All your worst decisions and best decisions started in the same exact place: with a thought. The match that lit the fuse was a soundtrack. The great news is that we can do something about that. A thought might show up uninvited—those are called *intrusive thoughts*—but it doesn't mean I have to entertain it.

Like an Instagram ad that shows up on my feed, I don't have to let that thought come in. I don't have to click on it, read it, and follow the link to whatever it's selling. For instance, let's say I suddenly think out of the blue, "I would be more popular if I was taller." That thought hits me like a rogue wave when I'm eating breakfast one morning. I'm momentarily caught off guard, but I eventually ask it our three questions:

Is it true? Is it helpful? Is it kind?

It's not true. No one has ever said to me, "I'd be your friend if you were an inch taller."

It's not helpful. Other than wearing a pair of shoes, I can't make myself taller. That thought won't help me change the situation.

It's not kind. I would never say to a friend, "You're too short to be popular," so why am I saying it to myself?

Instead of believing that thought, repeating it, and adding it to my playlist for the day, I can label it "broken soundtrack" and move on. Retiring that broken soundtrack is only the first step, though, because my brain wants something to think about. It's eager for another soundtrack to listen to.

That's where the second step comes in: replacing broken soundtracks with new ones.

I think about it for a minute and decide to replace "I would be more popular if I was taller" with "I'm the perfect height for me."

Do I believe it immediately? Maybe not. Maybe that broken soundtrack is persistent and keeps causing a fuss in my brain's front yard, trying to intrude on my life again. That's why in chapter 13 we'll talk about how important it is to repeat these new soundtracks. But for now I'm already in a better place than when I started because I'm actively choosing the thoughts I'm going to listen to all day.

"I'm the perfect height for me."

"My friends like me for me, not my height."

"My tallest friends slouch because they feel 'too tall.' Everyone is insecure about their height, not just me."

I might come up with three new soundtracks or 10, depending on how loud the broken one is that I'm retiring. Replacing the broken ones with new ones isn't even that complicated either. All you have to do is flip a coin.

11

You Should Flip It

Which would be harder for you: writing down the negative thoughts you have about yourself today, or writing down the positive thoughts you want to have about yourself someday?

If you're like me and most of my friends, the answer is obvious. Writing down positive thoughts is more difficult. The reason why is that you've heard those broken soundtracks so often that you have every lyric memorized.

"The Way I Loved You" by Taylor Swift is the song I listened to the most in 2021. According to Spotify data, I (L.E.) played it 94 times that year. If you asked me to write down the lyrics, that would be very easy. I could do that in my sleep. But what about a song I've only heard once or twice? Would I know each word as perfectly as "The Way I Loved You"? Definitely not.

The same thing happens with your thoughts. If you've listened to "No one really likes you, they're just being nice" a thousand times, you can recite it perfectly. You've got it memorized. That's not a problem, though, because we're going to use that to our advantage.

I want you to imagine a coin. One side is full of thoughts that aren't true, helpful, or kind. If you flipped it over, though, what would the other side say?

Take, for example, this broken soundtrack: "Everyone else has it all figured out."

Is that true? Nope.

Is it helpful? Nope.

Is it kind? Nope.

If we wrote down the opposite of that soundtrack, what would we write down? How about:

"No one has it all figured out."

"Lots of my friends don't have it all figured out."

"Part of being a student is learning to figure it out."

"It's OK that I still have lots of things to figure out."

"I have people in my life who are excited to help me figure it out."

"Even my parents don't have it all figured out."

Any one of those would be more encouraging than the broken soundtrack "Everyone else has it all figured out." And you didn't need to do a long creative exercise to figure it out. All you did was flip a coin and look at what was on the opposite side. Let's do a few more.

Broken soundtrack:
I will always feel this way.
(Flip that over.)
New soundtrack:
Feelings constantly change and I'll feel different tomorrow.

Broken soundtrack:
I can't be the best.
(Flip that over.)
New soundtrack:
I can be the best me.

Broken soundtrack:

This bad grade will ruin my entire life.

(Flip that over.)

New soundtrack:

One bad grade is just one bad grade.

Broken soundtrack:

You're not good enough.

(Flip that over.)

New soundtrack:

I get a little bit better at the things I care about every day.

You might not believe these new soundtracks at first, especially if you've been listening to a broken soundtrack for a long time, but you can do it. Imagine how much better you'll feel if every time you hear the soundtrack "This bad grade will ruin my entire life" you flip a coin and instead remind yourself, "One bad grade is just one bad grade."

I think the flip is the easiest way to replace your broken soundtracks with new ones, but it's not the only thing you can do. You can also borrow from the best.

12

There's Great Music Everywhere

The funny thing about soundtracks is that once you learn about them, you'll start to hear them everywhere. At school, at home, on the radio, in a movie—you'll find so many examples of soundtracks that other people are listening to.

Guess what that means? You have a lot to choose from. My dad calls that "borrowing from the best." Where does it say you have to sit down with a blank piece of paper and write out your own soundtracks without any help whatsoever? Let's make this an open-book exam.

Wouldn't it be a lot more fun to just turn on your listening ears—raise your hand if your parents said that to you when you were a kid—and start to find fresh soundtracks from other people?

To do that, break out those three F's we discussed in chapter 8: family, friends, and future.

Family

Does your family have any positive soundtracks you can borrow?

One of ours is "We talk to each other the way we talk to others." My mom has told me hundreds of times, "If you wouldn't talk to your friends that way, don't talk to your sister that way." It's a quick, short reminder that helps me (L.E.) remember to be kind to McRae.

Another one we use is "We're try-hards." That one started when another student accused me of being a "try-hard," as if trying my best was a bad thing. I thought, "You're right, I am a try-hard!" and it became a family soundtrack. Chances are, if your parents gave you this book, they have a few good soundtracks you can pick up. They might call them "family mottos" or "family sayings," but those are the same thing as soundtracks.

Not that every soundtrack a family has is perfect. Stephen Scoggins is a successful podcaster, and his dad used to say, "Scoggins don't get ahead, they get by." Talk about a soundtrack that isn't true, helpful, or kind! When Stephen grew up, he had to retire that and replace it with something new.[1]

Friends

Do your friends have any positive soundtracks you can borrow?

We all have friends who are dramatic and exhausting to be around, but we also have friends who lift us up. One night a small group of my friends all wrote encouraging statements on pictures of each other. It might seem like a small thing that someone wrote, "L.E. you're a bright light in my life." But that's more than a compliment—that's a soundtrack. The next time I feel like I'm not enough, what if I reminded myself, "I'm a bright light in Jadyn's life."

Think about the person on the group project who actually made it happen. What soundtracks did they say out loud to push the team forward? I bet they said something like, "We can do this!" or "Let's get this finished!" or "This is easy!" That last one is a soundtrack we say all the time in our marching band. When we have to do a dry run of a performance at 4:30 a.m. and it's cold outside and it's difficult to get motivated, we repeat that to each other: "This is easy!" The next time you run into a challenge in your own life, remember that soundtrack from that friend and tell yourself, "I can do this!"

Future

This one is a little different from those first two. With family and friends we were looking to borrow a soundtrack from our present life. With this one we're looking to create a soundtrack that will build our future life. If that sounds complicated, don't worry. It's not. All you have to do is ask yourself this question:

What do I want to be true in the future?

What are your dreams, goals, or aspirations? If your thoughts become your actions and your actions become your results, what are the results you want?

You could say, "I want to make the varsity cross-country team my senior year." That's something you want to be true in the future. That's the result. So now let's think about the actions and thoughts you'll need to get there. Here are some possible actions:

1. Ask the coach for a training plan.
2. Find friends who run a little faster and train with them.

3. Research the pace the varsity runners ran this year so you have a real target.
4. Find areas in your neighborhood where it's easy to run.
5. Get your homework done during study hall so you have extra time to run after school.

In a matter of minutes, you'd have some actions that would help you accomplish your result: making the team. Now, come up with a few soundtracks that will keep you motivated. You could write down:

1. My coach wants to help me.
2. Running with faster friends helps me get faster too.
3. I have time to get faster before tryouts.
4. I get work done during study hall.
5. I'll feel awesome after I do my training plan.

If you feel like you're bothering your coach by asking so many questions, you'll remember the soundtrack "My coach wants to help me." If you feel discouraged because your faster friends finish the run minutes before you do, you'll tell yourself the truth: "Running with faster friends helps me get faster too." If you feel like goofing off during study hall, you'll pause and think, "I get work done during study hall."

The right soundtracks will encourage you to do the action, which will mean you get the result in the future. And it all starts with asking one question:

What do I want to be true in the future?

Fun

We had to add a fourth F, *fun*, because without it you'll miss an amazing source of new soundtracks. What's a song lyric that encourages you? What's a movie quote that gets you fired up? What's a TV show that makes you think bigger about your own life? What's a YouTube channel that always makes you smile? The world is full of creative soundtracks, and you can borrow them from anywhere. So many of my friends have T-shirts that say "BELIEVE" from the show *Ted Lasso*. It's only one word, but who says soundtracks have to be long to be helpful?

Once you start looking for fun soundtracks, you're going to be surprised how easy they are to find.

If that feels like a lot to start with, I've got your back. There are seven true, helpful, and kind soundtracks you can borrow right in this book. These were carefully curated—fancy word—based on the unique challenges and opportunities we students face. We'll knock them out in a few micro chapters that will help you add them to your new playlist quickly.

Before we do, though, let's talk for a minute about the third step to tap into the superpower of mindset: *repeat*.

Repeat as Necessary

A funny thing happened 48 hours after my dad's book *Soundtracks* came out. People started sending him emails, DMs, and text messages saying that their new soundtracks "weren't working." They had retired their broken soundtracks. They had replaced them with new ones. But they were having a hard time believing their new thoughts. They worried that maybe there was something wrong with them, but the truth was a lot simpler than that: they just hadn't repeated the new ones yet.

Repeating your new soundtracks is the third step of the process, and if you skip it, you won't experience the real fun that happens when your thoughts turn into actions and your actions turn into results. Since the book had only been out for two days, new readers really hadn't had time to repeat their soundtracks often enough to believe them.

There are definitely instances where learning one new idea can change everything immediately. Have you ever had a friend change overnight? You thought you knew him, but then in a weekend he became a different person and returned to school moody, angry, and standoffish. His grades plummet, his attitude changes, and his friend circle is completely different.

It's easy in that moment to judge your friend, but what happens when you find out his parents are getting divorced? Doesn't your understanding of who he is and what he is going through change completely? Knowing that one idea—"My friend's parents are getting divorced"—would explain everything else in his life.

There are instances like that, where something happens overnight that forever changes your way of thinking. But there are other situations where it takes time to believe something new, especially when it comes to our soundtracks.

It's like any other goal in life. If you were struggling with calculus and said to me, "McRae, calculus is impossible," I might ask you, "How long have you been studying it?" If you answered, "Three weeks," I'd then ask, "How long did it take you to learn precalculus?" You would probably say, "Six months." (Both are hard subjects!)

Well, if it took you six months last time, it might take you six months this time—maybe even more because it's a tougher class.

Learning new things takes time, whether that's figuring out how to drive, how to speak French, or how to retire, replace, and repeat your soundtracks.

Broken soundtracks are persistent, especially if they started with something a person in authority told you. If a gym teacher told you that you'll never be athletic and then you listened to that broken soundtrack for three years without realizing it, you might need to do a little work to replace it.

That's where repeat comes in. We're not just going to write down a bunch of true, helpful, and kind soundtracks and hope they stick. We're going to find creative ways to stack the odds in our favor.

This Is Silly, but It Works

What do you think of when you hear words and phrases like *positive thinking*, *affirmations*, *mantras*, or *pep talks*?

Maybe you think about your grandmother who always had a piece of candy for you and a kind word. Maybe you think of a coach who had statements covering every wall in the locker room: "We can do this!" "Teamwork makes the dream work!" "There is no complaining in this house!" Maybe you think of a cheesy school assembly where someone enthusiastically told you about why you shouldn't Juul or drive under the influence.

A running joke in our family is that when my dad drops me off at school, he rolls down the car window and yells, "Try not to cyberbully anyone today, McRae!" He does this because he thinks it's funny (it's mildly humorous at best) and knows that most high schools are plastered with motivational posters giving us advice like that.

I don't know how you feel about positive thinking, but at some point in these next few chapters, you're going to feel silly. That's OK because everyone does when they first learn about the power of affirmations. This is maybe the cheesiest thing you'll find in this book save for all the dad jokes that someone who has the same last name as me keeps trying to slide in. I'm like a hockey goalie over here, blocking puns left and right. I hope you appreciate it.

Think of these next seven soundtracks as "starter soundtracks." More than likely, you'll also write your own based on your unique life situation. The girl from chapter 2 who was telling herself she was the slowest swimmer on the team could use a new soundtrack like, "I get a little better at swimming each practice." That would apply to her specifically but would feel a little strange if you weren't a swimmer.

But we individually selected these seven soundtracks for the situations every student faces. How did we pick them? Remember those boxes of soundtracks students wrote down? Remember the hundreds of real things that real students said? That's how. We sorted. We collated. We studied. We researched. We looked for patterns and similarities and the common thread between students of all ages. A long list became a shorter list became seven soundtracks.

These are seven that will help you start to build your new playlist regardless of your unique life situation.

Without further ado, here's Soundtrack 1!

14

SOUNDTRACK 1:

Enough Is a Myth

Why is this the very first new soundtrack I (L.E.) think you should start repeating to yourself? Because the number one most common word shared in that big box of broken soundtracks is *enough*.

Here's what students wrote down:

"I'm not pretty enough to fit in."

"I'm not popular enough."

"I'm not smart enough."

"I'm not happy enough."

"I'm not rich enough."

"I'm not good enough."

"I'm not strong enough."

"I'm not tall enough."

"I don't have enough friends."

"I'm not skinny enough despite how much I work out."

"I don't play piano well enough to major in it."

"I'm not balanced enough."

Have you ever heard any of those soundtracks? I think every student on the planet has experienced at least one of them. It's understandable, though, because *enough* sounds amazing, doesn't it?

Enough is full of promises.

If you get pretty enough, you'll never feel insecure again. If you get popular enough, you'll never feel lonely again. If you get smart enough, you'll never feel dumb again. If you get strong enough, you'll never feel weak again. If you get happy enough, you'll never feel sad again. If you get rich enough, you'll never feel inadequate again.

Who doesn't want that?

I want that! Are you telling me there's something I can do to never feel insecure, lonely, dumb, weak, sad, or inadequate? Sign me up!

There's only one problem though: that's a switch mentality. Remember in chapter 7, where we talked about the difference between a switch and a dial? A switch tells you that you can find one thing that will forever switch off every negative feeling, emotion, or situation. A dial tells you that sometimes life is stressful, sometimes the dial gets turned up high, but there are things we can do to turn it down.

Enough offers a promise it just can't keep. You'll never feel pretty enough, skinny enough, smart enough, popular enough, or anything else enough because enough doesn't exist. It's an undefined, unreachable, always changing standard that's impossible to achieve.

If you tell yourself that you'd feel popular enough if you got invited to that next party, guess what happens when the party is over? You start thinking about the next one. Enough isn't a finish line, it's a hamster wheel, and you never stop spinning if you chase it.

Plus, it's lying to you.

I've got some terrible but very honest news for you: You are going to feel sad sometimes. You are going to feel inadequate sometimes. You are going to feel afraid sometimes. That's not failure, that's life. We all go through ups and downs.

Your emotions are going to show up before stressful moments. That's just what they do. If you felt stressed out about the homecoming dance, do you

ENOUGH

ISN'T A FINISH LINE, IT'S A **HAMSTER WHEEL**, AND YOU NEVER STOP SPINNING **IF YOU CHASE IT.**

know what else you'll probably feel stressed out about? Prom. If you felt stressed out about prom, do you know what else you'll probably feel stressed out about? Your sorority formal in college.

That's when enough gets loud. It will tell you, "If I was popular enough, I wouldn't feel stressed out about homecoming, prom, or the winter formal." But that's not true, because enough is a myth.

So, the first soundtrack I want you to write down is exactly that: "Enough is a myth."

Every time you hear the word *enough* pop into your head, I want you to tell yourself, "Enough is a myth." Don't chase it. Don't give it your valuable time, energy, or creativity. Don't let the lie of enough distract you from a soundtrack that's true and a whole lot more fun: "I'm the best at being me." You are. Even if you don't feel like it sometimes, you're the best you because you're the only you. There are 7 billion people on the planet and there's only one you.

There's only one L.E. Acuff. Am I perfect? Nope. Do I have it all figured out? Of course not. Am I a continual work in progress? Without a doubt. But working on myself patiently is a lot different from running after enough.

Why? Because progress is possible, but enough is a myth.

15

SOUNDTRACK 2:

I'm Capable of More Than I Think

It's good to ask your loudest soundtracks the question "Is it true?" Despite our thoughts constantly telling us fables, it's so tempting to believe everything we think is true. But what happens when you ask that question and find a thought that's lying to you? What do you do then?

You replace it with a true thought, like the second soundtrack on our list: "I'm capable of more than I think."

I (McRae) didn't think I was capable of passing Biology. Guess what happened? I passed Biology.

I didn't think I was capable of passing Geometry. Guess what happened? I passed Geometry.

I bet next year my thoughts will tell me I'm not capable of passing Algebra 2. But guess what will happen? I'll pass Algebra 2.

How do I know that? Because I'm capable of more than I think—and so are you. Everyone is, because when it comes to our capabilities, our thoughts tend to draw the boundaries so much smaller than they really are. That's how fear works. Fear is afraid you'll get hurt, so it tries to protect you. It reminds me of a metaphor about a soccer field and a postage stamp that a writer named Ted Boccelli shared with my dad once.

Imagine if your life was a soccer field. Fear is worried you'll go out of bounds, so it tells you, "Don't go close to that sideline; stay at least 10 feet away." You pull back a little, thinking that will satisfy fear.

But fear doesn't quiet down once you give in to it. The next day it will tell you, "You know what, 10 feet away from the edge isn't enough. Better back up another 10 feet." You do, and maybe for a day, a week, or even a month fear is quiet.

But then one day when you think about doing something new or stepping out, fear says, "Twenty feet away from the edge is good, but what would be even better is 30 feet away from out of bounds." Foot

I'M CAPABLE OF MORE THAN I THINK— AND SO ARE YOU.

by foot, week by week, you keep taking steps away from some imaginary danger until you find yourself in the middle of the field, balancing on one foot in a patch of grass the size of a postage stamp.

Your capabilities are now small, constricted, and not nearly as fun as they were when you were a little kid and thought you could be an artist, an astronaut, a firefighter, or a famous YouTuber. But your thoughts aren't telling you the truth.

You're capable of more than you think. You're capable of tremendous things. Our generation is going to reshape the world. We're going to go to Mars. We're going to invent things no one has ever dreamed of. We're going to build businesses and families and ideas that future generations will write books about.

Despite what fear tells you, there's no telling how many amazing things you're really capable of.

Your "fake positivity meter" should be going off right now. Maybe the soundtrack "You're capable of more than you think" sounds an awful lot like "You can be anything you want in life." That one is fun to say, but unfortunately it's not true.

I'm probably not going to be in the Olympics. My sister L.E. didn't instantly become best friends with Millie Bobby Brown from *Stranger Things* when she met her at that photo event. My dad, despite writing books about positive thinking, isn't going to be in the NBA. He's 5'7". In the entire 75-year history of the NBA, there have only been nine players that height or shorter. I gotta be honest, I don't like his odds.

I think sometimes the reason we students don't trust motivational hype from parents, teachers, or guidance counselors is because it's just that—hype. It's not true. Let's keep this book honest: you can't be anything you want to be, but the good news is you get to be something real.

You get to be you.

You get to be 100 percent you.

And that person is capable of more than you think.

The next time fear tries to limit you, press play on that soundtrack. You've got a whole soccer field of life to explore—never settle for a postage stamp.

You're capable of more than you think.

16

SOUNDTRACK 3:

Be Brave Enough to Be Bad at Something New

I'm terrible at pole vaulting.

I'm the worst at driving a dirt bike.

I'm very mediocre at understanding German medieval poetry at a college level.

How do I know this?

Because I've never done any of those things. That's one of the simple rules of life that I think we can all agree on: we will be bad at things we've never done.

We understand that in our heads. We know it's true, but I'm always surprised at how often we forget it. There's a great temptation to beat ourselves up when we start doing something new and it doesn't instantly go well.

It took me (McRae) months to figure out the social dynamics of the high school cafeteria.

It took me an entire season to feel good about cross-country.

It took me almost a whole year to understand geometry.

Those are three very different activities, but do you know what they all have in common? I wanted to be better a whole lot faster. Maybe I didn't exactly want overnight success because I've heard so many adults preach against that, but I didn't want to stumble as much as I did. I didn't want to fumble my way through those early weeks and months as I was learning. I didn't want to make so many mistakes.

What helped, though, is that we have a soundtrack we use in our family when we have to do new things: "Be brave enough to be bad at something new."

What does that mean? It means I'm not surprised when I suck at something new. I should be terrible. That's exactly what's supposed to be happening. I've never done it before. I should be the worst I'll ever be at this task because it's brand-new to me.

For example, I'm not going to be good at filling out college applications. How do I know? Because

BE **BRAVE ENOUGH** TO BE **BAD** AT SOMETHING NEW.

JON ACUFF

#YourNewPlaylist

I've never done it! It will be my first time, and it will feel a little intimidating. I know my parents will help me. I know my teachers will help me. I know my big sister might even help me too.

More than that, though, I know that I'll help me by repeating this soundtrack: "Be brave enough to be bad at something new."

That simple sentence will save you from weeks of frustration. It will free you from internal judgment that demands instant perfection. It will give you the ability to learn new things without the kind of impossible expectations that get in the way.

We're at an age where almost everything is new. I haven't taken a single class in college yet. I haven't paid my own taxes. I haven't been in a serious dating relationship. I haven't picked a career. I haven't written wedding vows. I haven't chosen a city to live in. I haven't furnished an apartment . . . yet.

I'm going to. You will too. There's an entire world of new headed our way. When it gets here, I hope you'll say what I'm going to say:

"Be brave enough to be bad at something new."

17

SOUNDTRACK 4:

Fear Gets a Voice, Not a Vote

Fearless **is an amazing** Taylor Swift album, but is it true? Can you ever become fearless?

Is there something you can do that will forever remove fear from your life? Can you become so consistently brave that you never experience fear again? Is there an action, a mantra, or a soundtrack that will prevent fear from ever bothering you?

No.

That's classic switch thinking. When someone tells you that you can become fearless, they're setting you up for failure. Why? Because whenever you do something new or different in your life, there's going to be some fear stirred up. New adventures always come with new fears.

You might not remember it, but you were probably a little afraid the first time you rode the bus. On the very first day of kindergarten you had kindergarten-sized fears about what the day would hold: *Will my teacher be nice? Will I know where to sit on the bus? Will recess be fun?* Little you had little fears.

But guess what you did? You went to kindergarten. You pushed through the fears and realized you were capable of being a pretty awesome kindergartener.

No one reading this right now is still in kindergarten. I've never met a single 18-year-old who said, "Yeah, I'm on my thirteenth year of kindergarten. I've been held back a dozen times." We all got through our kindergarten fears.

Then we went to elementary school, and elementary-school-sized fears showed up: *Will I have someone to sit with at lunch? Will I be able to learn cursive? Will multiplication be a challenge for me?* You pushed through those fears, knocked out elementary school, and then headed to middle school. Guess what showed up at middle school?

Middle-school-sized fears.

At each new level of life, a new set of fears shows up. You were brave in kindergarten. You were brave in elementary school. You were brave in middle school. You might not have felt it at the time, but you did it. You didn't quit kindergarten because you were afraid. You didn't drop out of third grade because fractions were a challenge. You did it. Fear got a little loud but you pushed through. Why?

Because fear gets a voice, not a vote. That's soundtrack number 4.

What does it mean?

It means that fear is going to be there. It's going to be extra chatty sometimes, and that's OK. We can hear it. We can even learn from it. It's not necessarily a bad thing. It's a good warning signal at times.

Pretending fear doesn't exist isn't honest, and thinking we should never feel fear isn't helpful. We can acknowledge it, process it, and then make the best decision regardless of it. But we don't have to give fear a vote.

Fear doesn't get to sit at the head of the table and tell us what to do.

Fear doesn't get to drive the car.

Fear doesn't get to choose our actions or adventures.

That's why one of our Acuff family soundtracks is "Fear gets a voice, not a vote."

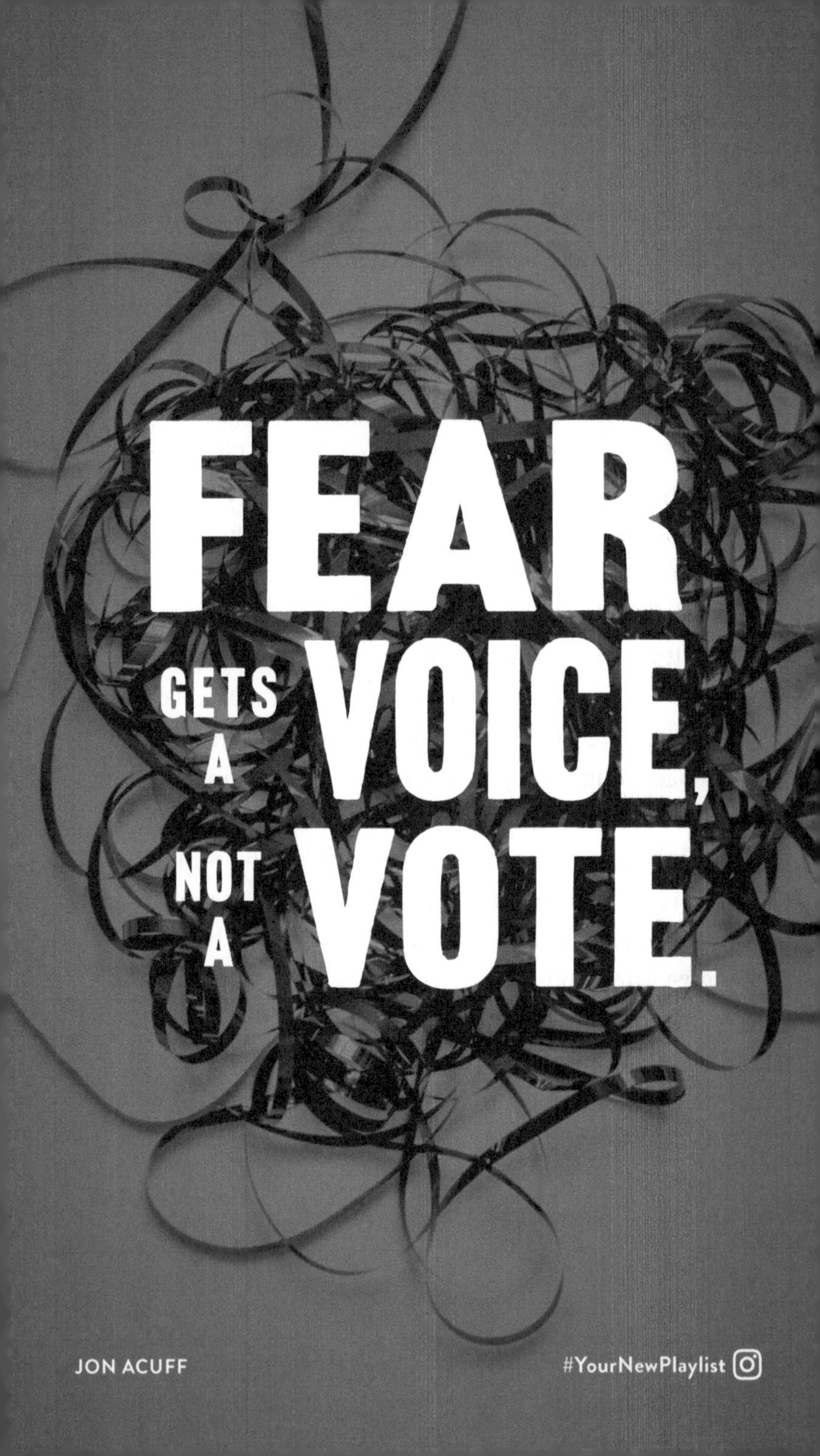
FEAR
GETS A VOICE,
NOT A VOTE.
JON ACUFF
#YourNewPlaylist

The first time I (McRae) went to cross-country practice, I had practice-sized fears. Would I be the slowest one there? Would I know how to do it? Would I need to walk more than everyone else? Would I know anyone on the team? Would people be nice to someone who was starting as a sophomore instead of as a freshman? I had a lot of fearful questions about that practice.

Fear had a voice in that moment, which is appropriate, but it didn't get a vote. Fear didn't get to tell me, "Don't go to cross-country practice. You should quit the team. Stay home." Fear didn't get to sit at the head of the table, bang a gavel, and rule on that decision. Instead, I went to cross-country practice, struggled for a few weeks, and then got over those fears.

Guess what happened when I ran my first meet? I had meet-sized fears (which makes it sound like I'm afraid of hamburgers). Even though I had beaten my practice-sized fears, when I leveled up to a race, there was just different fear there. I didn't beat myself up and think, "I should be fearless by now!" Instead I thought, "Oh, that's right, when I do new things, new fear shows up."

And that's OK, because fear gets a voice, not a vote. I pushed through and ran my first meet. By the second or third one, the meet-sized fears were mostly gone. I have a sneaking suspicion that when I sign up for my first 10K, I'll have 10K-sized fears. And if I run a half marathon, I'll have half-marathon-sized fears. And if I run a marathon . . . well, you see where I'm going.

When fear shows up, so do I.

But what would happen if I believed the broken soundtrack "If I was fast enough, then I'd never feel nervous before a race"? I would feel like a failure before every race. I'd never be fast enough to shut fear up. There's not an official minute-per-mile time that makes fear say, "Ohhh, McRae runs a seven-minute mile. I'd better leave her alone for the rest of her life."

If we gave fear a vote, we'd never leave the house. The doorbell would be terrifying. Each test would be a mountain, not just an exam. Each conversation with a friend would be a chance to say something stupid that could ruin everything. Fear tends to exaggerate. When it's put in power it tends to make some really small, really safe, really boring decisions.

FEAR DOESN'T GET TO CHOOSE OUR ACTIONS OR ADVENTURES.

That's not the kind of life you're going to lead.

You're going to do new things. A lot of them! You'll make new friends. Take new classes. Try new hobbies. Move to new cities. Visit new colleges. Date new people. Get new jobs. I don't know if you're Gen Z or Y or whatever the latest term is, but what we should all really be called is "Generation New." People our age are going to do more new things in a month than our parents do in an entire year!

I don't want us to miss that because fear tries to shut things down before they even get started. That's why it's so important to tap into the superpower of mindset right now. And it's a lot easier to do that when you remember:

Fear gets a voice, not a vote.

18

SOUNDTRACK 5:

I'm Just Getting Started!

Not every soundtrack I (L.E.) will recommend you repeat to yourself will end with an exclamation point, but this one needs it.

You can't quietly say, "I'm just getting started." This one needs to be shouted, even if it's just in your car on the way to school or in your bedroom all alone. This is a true statement that should be fired up into the air with the urgency of a bottle rocket on the Fourth of July.

I'm just getting started!

My dad would argue that you can say this

soundtrack at any age. After all, he didn't write his first book until he was 34 and didn't start his first business until he was 40.

There are even people in their seventies and eighties who will take his online challenges to accomplish a goal. I love that. I think it's great that our grandparents are still trying new things and going on new adventures.

But let's be honest for a second: when you're a teenager or in your twenties, you're the only one truly at the starting line. You have 60, 70, maybe even 80 years of runway ahead of you if Elon Musk invents some superfood that makes living to 100 easy.

We are just getting started!

There's a "too late" epidemic that tries to tell us that we've already missed our best opportunities. That because we didn't start playing softball when we were a toddler or get serious about our studies when we were seven or join the drama club when we were eight that we've run out of time.

That's exactly how I felt when I first joined the swim team when I was nine years old. My soundtracks back then said, "This is awful. I can't do this. I'm going to go home and tell Mom that I'm quitting." Part of the reason I felt that way was because there were five-year-olds at the practice. I thought, "I'm already four years behind the other

WE'RE JUST GETTING STARTED!

kids who are my age. I should have learned how to swim competitively when I was younger. I'm too late!"

That's garbage.

I pushed through with the help of my mom, who constantly said, "Be brave enough to be bad at something new," and eventually I made the state swimming championship in high school.

It wasn't too late for me, and it's not too late for you.

We're just getting started!

You've got your entire life ahead of you. Don't let the lie that it's too late steal that from you.

Whisper it if you must. Write it quietly on a piece of paper and stick it on your bathroom mirror if that helps. But for the moments when you feel like you've blown it, like you've missed your window or made some mistake you can never come back from, don't be afraid to get a little loud.

Tell yourself the truth.

I'm just getting started!

SOUNDTRACK 6:

People in the Game Always Get Criticized by People in the Stands

The ~~first draft~~ of this soundtrack was "No one is looking at me," but I (L.E.) realized that one is only true-ish.

It's true that in most situations you'll face as a student, no one is looking at you. No one at the mall is looking at you. No one in the cafeteria is looking at you. No one in your study hall is looking at you. No one at the sleepover is looking at you. No one at church is looking at you.

I guarantee your parents have said some version of that statement to you at one time or another. Maybe you were stressed out about what to wear to school or if your hair looked good or if your sneakers were old and lame. In that moment, chances are your mom said, "Stop overthinking everything. No one is watching you."

She's right, especially these days. Fewer people are watching us than ever before. Why? Because they're all on their phones. You could walk through the halls of your high school in a gorilla suit and most of your classmates wouldn't even notice because they're looking at their phones.

No one is looking at you.

That's true-ish. Where that idea breaks down is when you decide to be more than average. No one is watching you if you're average. If you're in a crowd, doing the same things everyone else is doing, no one even sees you. How could they? You fade into a sea of other people. But if you decide to step up, speak up, and stand out, do you know what's going to happen?

People are going to watch you.

When you're unique, brave, different, bold—pick any word that means "not average"—people can't help but notice. They're going to look at you. They're going to watch you. And when they do, sometimes they're going to criticize you. That's not because you've failed or done something wrong. That's just the ticket price for doing something awesome.

I didn't have a single one-star review until I wrote this book with my dad and McRae. A stranger never went on Amazon and said, "L.E. is not very good at marching band, she's terrible at AP English, and she's not that great at parallel parking." No one ever criticized my average life. But guess what's going to happen when this book comes out?

Someone is going to look at me. Someone is going to notice me. More than that, someone is going to notice this book and not like it. Someone is going to pick it apart. Someone is going to write a one-star review. That's fine, though, because *people in the game always get criticized by people in the stands.*

Whether your game is to become an Eagle Scout, run for class president, work on your back tuck for a year so that you make the cheerleading squad, or something completely different, when you move beyond average you're going to face a little criticism.

That's how adventures work. People who are too afraid to go on one always criticize people who are too brave to stay in the stands. And if you're reading this book, that's you.

Most people don't make it this far in books. Most students don't read books about changing their

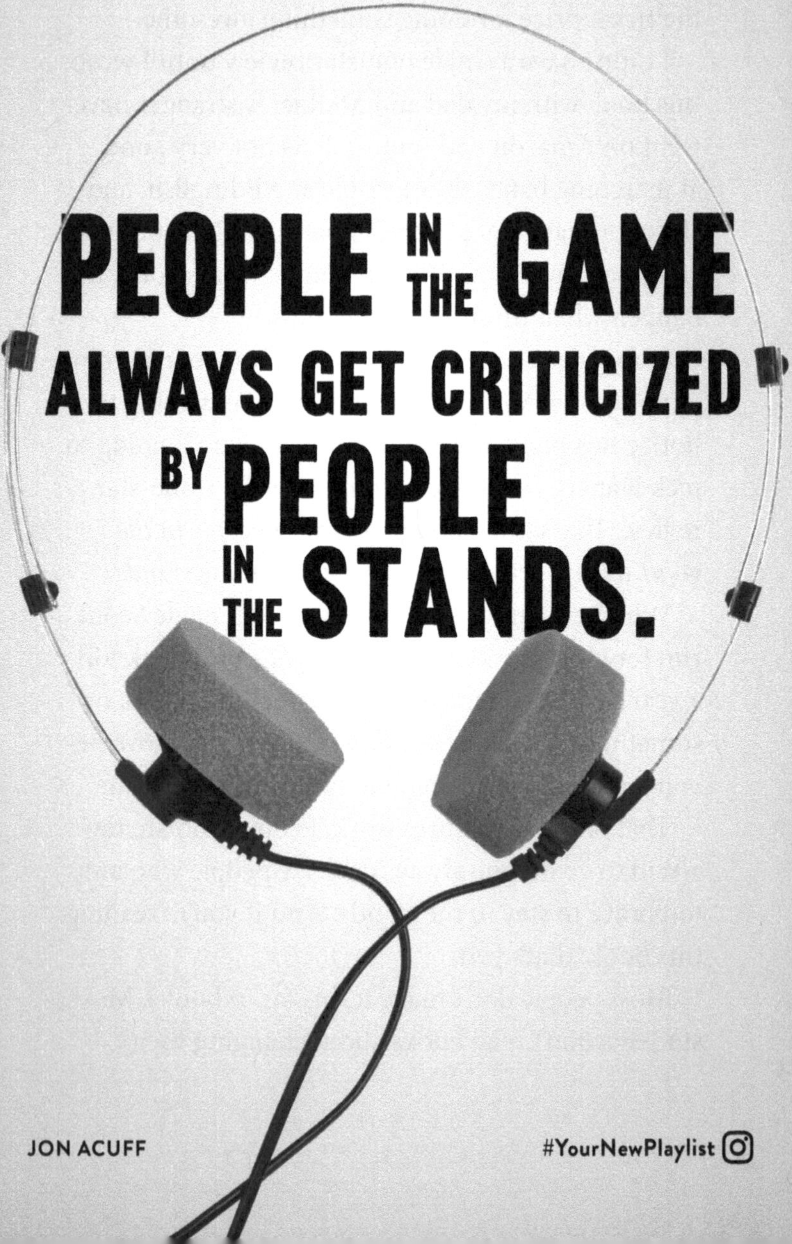
PEOPLE IN THE GAME
ALWAYS GET CRITICIZED
BY PEOPLE
IN THE STANDS.
JON ACUFF
#YourNewPlaylist

mindset. Most people don't dare to be anything but average.

But we're not most people.

The game is waiting for someone just like you. When you join it, don't worry about a little criticism. Just remember:

People in the game always get criticized by people in the stands.

20

SOUNDTRACK 7:

Everyone Feels Like This

I (McRae) made a complete list of all the students I know who have life all figured out:

1.
2.
3.
4.
5.

Did you recognize any of those names? Me either, because they don't exist. Perfect students, just like that idea of *enough*, are a myth. And everyone feels like this.

What's "this"?

Confused. Happy. Scared. Lonely. Mad. Hurt. Excited. Hopeful. Unpopular. Worried. Glad.

"This" is every emotion and feeling you can imagine. When you're young, you feel all of those things, often before you even get out of bed in the morning. The worst part is that at our age, our bodies betray us.

Do you know why you sometimes overreact to insignificant problems? Because your body is dumping gobs of hormones into your bloodstream. (Sorry to get so technical with that scientific term "gobs.") If our parents had the chemical makeup we've got right now combined with brains that aren't even completely formed, they'd be running around like maniacs.

Sometimes we don't give ourselves enough credit just for making it through the day with these wild machines we're in charge of. It's like someone handed us the keys to a Lamborghini and then said, "Good luck learning how to drive that thing!"

We feel all the things, which is fine, but then we think we're the only one who does. We assume it's just us. None of our friends feel like this. They've got it all together. They've got it all figured out. We're the only ones with a hurricane of emotions. Only we're not.

Everyone feels like this.

Not just you. Not just a handful of students in

your neighborhood. Not just a few of your friends. Everyone.

Right now there's a sophomore in Boise, Idaho, who thinks she's the only one who is worried about college. Right now there's a 21-year-old in Tallahassee, Florida, who thinks he's the only one who doesn't love his major. Right now there's a senior in Kyrkjebyrkjeland, Norway, who thinks life is over because he got cut from the bobsled team. (That's a real town in Norway, and I assume every Norwegian high school has a bobsled team.)

"This" is universal.

Everyone feels like this.

And here's the best news—and a bonus new soundtrack for you: feelings aren't forever.

Add that one to the list of new soundtracks you say. Feelings aren't forever. They usually aren't even for a whole day. Did you ever feel different at the end of the day than you did at the beginning? Did you ever feel different hour to hour or maybe even minute to minute? That's because feelings aren't forever.

 **FEELINGS AREN'T FOREVER.**

Of course they'll try to convince you that they are. A bad feeling will say, "No one else feels like this, and you'll always feel like this." But those are lies. Everybody feels like this, and feelings aren't forever.

The next time some broken soundtrack tries to tell you that you're the only one, don't listen. Retire that thought, replace it with the truth, and repeat it so often that it becomes automatic.

Don't just do that with "Everyone feels like this" either. Use all the new soundtracks we've talked about in these chapters:

Soundtrack 1: Enough is a myth.

Soundtrack 2: I'm capable of more than I think.

Soundtrack 3: Be brave enough to be bad at something new.

Soundtrack 4: Fear gets a voice, not a vote.

Soundtrack 5: I'm just getting started!

Soundtrack 6: People in the game always get criticized by people in the stands.

Soundtrack 7: Everyone feels like this.

Maybe you came up with your own new soundtrack as you've been reading. Even better! Write that one down too. Put all of these in your phone. Scribble them on your bathroom mirror with

SOUNDTRACK 1:
ENOUGH IS A MYTH.

SOUNDTRACK 2:
I'M CAPABLE OF MORE THAN I THINK.

SOUNDTRACK 3:
BE BRAVE ENOUGH TO BE BAD AT SOMETHING NEW.

SOUNDTRACK 4:
FEAR GETS A VOICE, NOT A VOTE.

SOUNDTRACK 5:
I'M JUST GETTING STARTED!

SOUNDTRACK 6:
PEOPLE IN THE GAME ALWAYS GET CRITICIZED BY PEOPLE IN THE STANDS.

SOUNDTRACK 7:
EVERYONE FEELS LIKE THIS.

JON ACUFF

#YourNewPlaylist

a dry erase marker. Jot them in a journal, on a Post-it note, or across the sky if you own one of those planes that spells things out with smoke.

Make it as easy as possible to remember what's true about you and your life. Some research even suggests it's helpful to say soundtracks like these out loud in front of the mirror first thing in the morning and last thing before bed. If that feels ridiculous, it's only because it is in fact ridiculous. But if it works, if it helps you tap into the superpower of mindset, maybe it's time to get a little ridiculous.

You've learned the three questions to ask each broken soundtrack. You discovered the difference between a switch and a dial. You figured out how to create your own soundtracks. You've made so much progress, but I must warn you: Fear won't give up that easily. Doubt won't go down without a fight.

If we want to really tap into the superpower of mindset, we have to go on the offense. That's exactly what we're going to do in the next three chapters. You're about to learn how to:

1. Change the sound of the song.
2. Gather evidence.
3. Use symbols to make soundtracks stick.

21

Change the Sound
of the Song

Do you know why you think every thought you have is true? Do you know why you're so quick to trust them? Do you know why they've been playing for years without your even noticing?

Because your thoughts sound like you.

Have you ever realized that? The soundtracks you listen to, even the ones that are really broken and are obviously lies, are delivered in your own voice. When you hear "You'll never find a boyfriend," it sounds familiar and trustworthy because it's in the voice you've heard the most your entire life: your own.

I (L.E.) sound like me to me.

McRae sounds like McRae to McRae.

You sound like you to you.

We get used to the things we hear over and over again. If you live near train tracks, guess what you eventually don't notice anymore? Loud trains. If you live in a busy city, guess what you eventually don't notice anymore? City noise. If you live in a flight path, guess what you eventually don't notice anymore? Planes. That's why so many soundtracks in our heads play without ever being noticed.

But what if it didn't have to be that way? What if you could go on the offense and change that before fear got loud again? You can, and it's actually pretty fun. All you do is change the sound of the soundtrack.

Think about it like changing the voice of Alexa, Siri, or the Google Assistant. Alexa, for instance, can speak to you with an American, British, or Australian accent—or even like Samuel L. Jackson. Changing a simple setting changes everything. The same is true when it comes to your soundtracks.

If a broken soundtrack you're listening to was delivered in the voice of a villain, you wouldn't trust it. If you heard "You'll never find a boyfriend" in the voice of Thanos from the Avengers movies, you wouldn't listen to it. You'd probably think, "That's not true. It's weird that Thanos is focused on my dating life instead of trying to destroy the universe, but regardless, I'm ignoring that."

If Voldemort was the one saying you won't get into college, you wouldn't believe that soundtrack.

If President Snow, the bad guy from the Hunger Games series, was the one telling you that your parents' divorce was your fault, you wouldn't accept that.

If the voice sounded like an enemy, you'd recognize it as such. It wouldn't take long either. Within a few seconds you'd see it for what it is, stop listening to it, and think about something else.

So today, pick your accent. Change the sound of your song to one that makes it easy to recognize and dismiss. You don't need to deep dive into your Alexa settings, just choose what works best for you.

Maybe you don't need to imagine a villain. Maybe you need to imagine broken soundtracks with a southern accent. Maybe you live in New Jersey and every time you hear someone from Mississippi speak, you laugh at how unusual their country drawl sounds. Or maybe it's the reverse. You live in Mississippi and New Jersey accents crack you up. Fuhgeddaboudit! (Dad joke that slipped through the cracks.)

Maybe it's more personal for you. Maybe you have a cousin who studied in France for a semester and

MAKE A SOUNDTRACK SILLY IF YOU WANT TO STOP LISTENING TO IT.

came home with a thin pencil mustache, a beret, and a phony accent that was ridiculous. Think of that one.

Come up with the most exaggerated, most obvious accent, and then decide that the next time a broken soundtrack gets loud you'll hear it that way. Make a soundtrack silly if you want to stop listening to it. Fear won't know what hit it. Imagine fear accidentally inhaling a bit of helium from a balloon. It gets madder and madder as it tries to convince you not to try out for the Model UN, but its voice just keeps getting higher and higher.

"What's happening to me? Stop this! Take me seriously!"

Only you wouldn't. You'd never let that broken soundtrack run the show again because what was once a loud, threatening soundtrack is now a tiny little mouse of a voice chirping at you angrily.

And no one wants to listen to that, especially when the evidence tells us that we don't even have to.

22

Gather Evidence

"Fear comes free, hope takes work."

If you ever became an official member of the Acuff family, that's a soundtrack you'd hear often.

Some others include:

"Early is on time."

"We get what we get and we don't pitch a fit."

And a personal favorite:

"That's not where shoes live."

McRae hears that last one a lot more often than I do because I (L.E.) am a perfect kid and never leave my shoes in the middle of the kitchen, but what can you do?

None of those need any extra explanation. "Early is on time" is about showing up 10 minutes early

EVERYWHERE we go. "We get what we get and we don't pitch a fit" is a greatest hit from our childhood that was mostly said when a restaurant didn't have chicken fingers and a tantrum was apparently not the solution. And shoes don't live in front of the fridge, on the stairs, in the living room, or really anywhere else but our closets.

But "Fear comes free, hope takes work"? That one needs a little backstory.

I won't bore you with the science, because you get enough of that in the classroom, but basically your brain is hardwired for negativity. Your brain tends to do three things that aren't super helpful:

1. It lies about your memories.
2. It confuses fake trauma with real trauma.
3. It believes what it already believes.

That's why it's so easy to remember something dumb you did and so hard to remember something good. Has that ever happened to you? In the middle of a French test your brain will say, "I can't believe that six months ago your friend left you off her 'I'm so thankful post' on Thanksgiving. I mean, she included photos of everyone at the lunch table except you. You weren't even mentioned in the caption.

What did you do? Want to think about that for a while and maybe fail this French exam?"

In moments like that, did you have to ask your brain to do that? Did you have to work hard to think about something stupid you said, or did that soundtrack just start playing on its own? I have a guess as to what you're saying right now.

That's how broken soundtracks work, and here's the reason:

Fear comes free, hope takes work.

You don't have to look for fear. It will find you on its own.

You don't have to seek out stress. It will seek you out.

You don't have to search out doubt. It will search you out.

Hope, on the other hand, takes effort.

Positive thinking takes practice.

Self-belief takes intentionality.

Tapping into the superpower of mindset is not accidental; it's always on purpose, and it starts by gathering evidence.

How to Gather Evidence

I (L.E.) almost didn't make the high school marching band my freshman year.

I played trumpet in middle school, but the Franklin High Band was a completely different animal. They practice 25 hours a week, compete in national tournaments, and function like a military machine.

The reason I almost didn't get a dot, which means a place in the marching band show that year, was because of Alaska. My family took an Alaskan cruise the summer before my freshman year and I missed band camp. If you've never done high school band, you're probably imagining a fun summer getaway for band nerds to go to the beach and bond. If only.

Band camp consists of 12-hour days spent constantly moving and learning that season's new show. Which I didn't get to do because I missed the entire thing. When I came back and tried to jump into band practice, I was lost. I felt like I was the only trumpet player who didn't know the steps, didn't know the music, and didn't know if I'd even make the cut.

Everyone around me had a head start, and while it was hard to catch up, it wasn't impossible. I put in the work, and by the end of the summer I was exactly where I needed to be. I got a dot and made the band!

Do you know what fear will never remind me of? That moment.

BROKEN SOUNDTRACKS ERASE PAST SUCCESS AND PROMISE FUTURE FAILURE.

Fear will never call to mind the time I made the band. It will never remind me of the group project we all got an A on. It will never remind me of the difficult conversation I had with a friend that ended up working out.

Broken soundtracks don't remind you of your accomplishments.

If anything, they do just the opposite. They trot out one of the most toxic "absolute" words we talked about way back in chapter 4: *never*.

You've *never* faced a test this hard.

You've *never* achieved anything.

You've *never* done anything difficult.

Broken soundtracks erase past success and promise future failure. The way we defeat that is by creating a "hard list."

What's that, you ask?

It's exactly what it sounds like—a list of hard things you achieved.

For example, you could write down:

1. I managed to peacefully visit both Mom's and Dad's houses last Christmas even though it was the first one after their divorce.
2. I made the high school marching band.
3. I got the role I wanted in the play.
4. I made a new friend on the first day of school.
5. The manager at my grocery store job said I did a good job stocking the shelves.
6. I didn't have an argument with my little brother for an entire road trip.
7. I won the Frisbee distance toss in fourth grade.

Wait a second . . . maybe you're in college and fourth grade was 12 years ago. Does that count?

Of course it does. It all counts.

Broken soundtracks don't have a time limit on what they'll remind you of. For example, my dad once ruined a surprise party, and just the other day he was feeling terrible about that memory. He had accidentally told a coworker's husband about the party, and Stacy, his coworker, was furious at him. When my parents went to the party later that night, Stacy stopped the music as my dad walked in, then pointed at him and announced to everyone, "This

is Jon Acuff. He's the one who ruined this party."
Awkward.

He regrets it. Who wouldn't? But there's an even bigger problem: that happened nearly 20 years ago. Two decades after his silly mistake, my dad's brain still says, "Here's a classic song—a real deep cut. Want to listen to this one today?" Twenty years later!

Broken soundtracks don't fight fair, and neither will we.

So, if you've made it this far in the book—so close to that $20!—I dare you to do a little homework. The next time you do something good, whether it's something really big or incredibly small, I want you to open a note on your phone or a page in your journal and write "Hard List" at the top. Then I want you to write down what it was you did. Maybe even add a date to that moment to make it even more specific.

Why write it down? Because you're going to forget.

McRae forgot she conquered Biology her freshman year. When she was struggling with Geometry her sophomore year, a broken soundtrack tried to tell her she had never taken a class this hard. Only she had. She'd just forgotten to put it on her hard list.

Gather evidence that reminds you how capable you really are. To tap into the superpower of mindset, tap into your list as many times as you need to.

FEAR COMES FREE, HOPE TAKES WORK.

JON ACUFF

#YourNewPlaylist

Fear comes free, hope takes work.

Put in the work and then the next time fear tries to tell you that you can't do something, bust out your list. You've got evidence right there to remind you of the truth. If you read the next chapter you might even have a symbol that helps you with that too.

23

Get Sticky with a Symbol

I (L.E.) own a hatebird.

Technically, the small tropical bird that lives in the corner of my bedroom is a lovebird, but since she only likes me and hates every other member of my family, hatebird feels like a better description for her.

Her name is Buddy and she's four years old, which means she has about a thousand years of life left. (Heads up to any parents who are reading this: Think twice before giving your kids a pet bird. They live FOREVER. If you want a small-commitment pet that is fun on Christmas but gone by the Fourth of July, a hamster is a much safer bet.)

Buddy is not the only unusual thing in my bedroom at home. There's also a massive baby blue and white skimboard. There's an electric guitar hanging on one wall. There's a series of plants in various stages of death and the school clutter that every student has. But what dominates the room is my photo wall, a collection of hundreds of pictures that fill the largest wall.

Like an old-school version of a Pinterest board, the wall isn't accidental. Every one of those photos was picked on purpose. Some are of friends I love. Some are places I want to visit. Some are movies that mean a lot to me, like *Back to the Future*, or TV shows I'll watch on repeat, like *The Office*. It's a personal collection of images that starts my day with a little bit of inspiration and ends my night with a little bit of encouragement.

I get a lot out of my photo wall, and it turns out there's a reason.

Those photos are not just photos. Those photos are symbols, and symbols are a powerful way to make new soundtracks stick.

What Nike and Lululemon Know

Is Lululemon big at your school?

Is Nike popular?

Maybe where you live it's Carhartt or Champion, Adidas or Vineyard Vines. Styles differ from town to town, but one thing remains the same: a logo matters. The Nike swoosh isn't just a creative illustration, it's a symbol. And it means you're in the know. You have money or taste. You're aware of what's cool, and by wearing it you're cool too.

Symbols and the meanings we attach to them are powerful tools for remembering stories about our world and even for replaying our soundtracks. If you want to tap into the superpower of mindset and make your new soundtracks really sticky, the easiest way is to attach a symbol to them.

If that sounds complicated, I promise it's not. You're probably already surrounded by symbols right now. Do you have your driver's license? If you do, I bet your keychain has something unique attached to it. Do you bring a backpack to school? Do you have a button on it, a lanyard clipped to it, or anything else that makes it *your* backpack and not someone else's? Look at your nightstand. Do you have an old copy of a program from a play you were in, a ticket stub from a college football game, a necklace your aunt gave you? All of those are symbols, objects that hold a memory you don't want to lose.

You might not have thought you picked them on

purpose, but there is meaning behind every item you've included in your life.

If you want to get the most out of your new playlist, it helps to create a few symbols. It's not difficult. All you do is take a new soundtrack, like "I can do hard things," and find a symbol for it that is:

1. Simple
2. Personal
3. Visible

Why does it need to be simple? Because if it's complicated, you won't really use it. My sister McRae sometimes struggles with perfectionism. My mom will ask her to clean her room, and two hours later she'll come back to find McRae carefully organizing her sock drawer with a system that divides the socks according to color, thickness, and purpose. (Slight exaggeration, but not much.) This frustrates my mom because she really just wanted to be able to see McRae's floor and she knows McRae will never use that sock system again. It's too difficult. It has too many steps.

The first thing you want to do is make your symbol *simple*. That's why my dad has a pinecone on his desk. It doesn't get much simpler than that. Why is

IF YOU WANT YOUR SOUNDTRACK TO STICK, YOUR SYMBOL MUST BE:

1. SIMPLE

2. PERSONAL

3. VISIBLE

JON ACUFF

#YourNewPlaylist 📷

it there? Well, a few years ago we were all going on a family vacation to Jackson Hole, Wyoming. Unfortunately, the week after that trip, my dad had a deadline for a book manuscript.

Normally that would mean he'd be physically present for the trip but mentally absent. Have your parents ever pulled that move—like they are there, but they're not really there? It usually means they've got a stressful soundtrack playing on repeat and can't even hear what's going on around them. This time, however, since my dad had been researching the power of soundtracks, he decided to approach the trip differently.

A few weeks before we left, he wrote "Don't miss it" on a Post-it note and stuck it on the window in his office. When I say your symbol should be simple, I mean it. Everyone reading this can write something encouraging on a scrap of paper. That's a symbol and it's not hard to do.

He wrote "Don't miss it" because—and this is going to blow your mind, I know—he didn't want to miss the trip. He read that note hundreds of times before we left, repeated it out loud to himself dozens of times, and committed it to memory. (It's three words, so it was probably pretty easy.) Weeks later, when we were walking around Jackson Hole, he stopped to pick up a pinecone on the street.

The pattern on it was completely different from the pinecones we have back home in Nashville. The only way he was able to even notice something as small and insignificant as a pinecone is that he was present. Why was he present, even though he had a big book deadline on the horizon? Because he listened to the soundtrack "Don't miss it." At the end of the trip, he brought that pinecone back 1,636 miles (googled that) and put it on his desk because he knew that wouldn't be the last time he was tempted to be distracted. Now, in addition to the note, his pinecone is a symbol to remind him, "Don't miss it." That's simple.

The second thing your symbol needs to be is *personal*. Your sister's symbol won't work for you. Your mom's symbol won't work for you. Your dad's symbol won't work for you. It has to be personal to who you are and what soundtracks you care about.

McRae has a trunk she takes to camp each summer. It's covered with stickers that capture all the adventures she's been on over the years. It sits at the foot of her bed, and she sees it dozens of times a day. What does it mean to her?

It means, "I do brave things."

The camp she goes to is a two-week camp hundreds of miles away from our house. It's also the kind of camp that kids go to from the time they

start kindergarten through their senior year of
high school. People don't tend to go for the first
time when they're in the eighth grade. A broken
soundtrack told McRae, "It's too late to start going to
camp." But she didn't listen, because she does brave
things. Last summer she even upped the ante and
signed up for the wilderness portion, where instead
of sleeping in classic cabins you actually hike for
days at a time and sleep under the stars.

McRae does brave things. Her trunk reminds her
of that. That's what it means to her. Know what it
means to me? Nothing. It's just a trunk. It's not my
symbol, it's hers.

Make sure that whatever symbol you use is personal to you. Want an easy way to double check that
it is? Find something that's so personal that someone
else might find it a little silly or even weird. Let's be
honest, a grown man putting a pinecone in a little
plastic bag and transporting it across the country
in his briefcase is strange. Who cares though? We're
not using symbols to impress people. We're using
them to tap into the superpower of mindset. Keep it
personal.

Last but not least, your symbol needs to be *visible*.
You can't miss McRae's trunk.
You can't miss my photo wall.

You can't miss the pinecone in the bowl on the corner of my dad's desk.

The final key to a good symbol is that you see it often. Stick it on the corner of your bathroom mirror. Hang it on the wall by your bed. Attach it to your keychain. Carry it in your pocket for particularly stressful days.

Sports teams do this all the time. Whether it's the fictional soccer team in *Ted Lasso* slapping the bright yellow BELIEVE sign before a game or the Clemson Tigers football team rubbing their famous rock before they take the field, high performance athletes keep their symbols visible and so should you.

If you don't know where to start, try taking one of the soundtracks on your new playlist and attaching it to one of these symbols:

1. *A pair of shoes.* NBA players write encouraging notes on their shoes, which are . . . soundtracks. Got a big game coming up or a test that feels monstrous? Write "You've got this!" somewhere on your cleats or inside a pair of Doc Martens.

2. *Headphone case.* Want an easy reminder that you get to choose the thoughts you listen to? Every time you take out your headphone case, tell yourself, "My thoughts, my choice."

3. *Phone lock screen.* Know what you're going to see a hundred times today? Your phone lock screen. Turn it into a symbol with a photo of something that reminds you of an important soundtrack.

4. *A piece of jewelry.* When you turn 16 in our family, my grandmother gives you a bracelet. I haven't taken mine off for three years. Every time I see it, I'm reminded of the soundtrack "My grandma loves me and is proud of the person I'm becoming." Use a necklace, earrings, bracelet, nose ring, or any piece of jewelry to set a soundtrack in place.

5. *A rock.* Jewelry costs money. Do you know what's free? Rocks. The next time your family drags you on a difficult hike in a national park because your mom is obsessed with national parks, grab a small rock from the view up top. It will remind you, "I can do hard things."

6. *A good grade.* In the last chapter we talked about gathering evidence, and this is one example. When you do well on a test, take a screen shot of that grade and keep it handy in your phone. When the next test rolls around and a broken soundtrack tries to tell you, "You never get good grades," flip through your collection of screen shots to tell yourself the truth.

7. *A favorite Instagram account.* Although it's easy to get sucked into the negative side of social media, there's a lot of good there too. Make a short list of your favorite accounts, the ones that motivate you every time you see them. When you've got five free minutes in study hall, make a quick lap through them as a form of instant encouragement.

8. *A seashell.* This is essentially a fancy rock. They might be a little harder to acquire if the ocean is a long way from where you live, but a piece of the beach always reminds me how big the world really is. When my problems feel massive, a seashell makes them feel smaller.

9. *A T-shirt.* Someone once gave my parents a Yanni T-shirt as a present. If you don't know who Yanni is, please google him immediately. Prepare to be dazzled by his hair, his mustache, and his music. The T-shirt is airbrushed, and Yanni's long hair looks like it's rippling across the front of the shirt in Panama City Beach glory. I think it's funny. When I wear it to bed at night or around the house on the weekend, I instantly smile. Your symbol and soundtrack don't have to be serious and heartfelt. "I like to laugh" is a good soundtrack. The shirt makes me laugh. Therefore, Yanni.

10. *A peach pit carved into a monkey.* Don't have that exact one lying around your house? You must not know Grandy, my great-grandfather. I think by law great-grandfathers have to whittle in their free time. Grandy loves carving peach pits into monkeys. I have one in my room, and it reminds me of him. Can something that small and insignificant be a symbol? Definitely. Anything can, as long as it's simple, personal, and visible.

I hope something on that list jumps out at you. If it does, awesome! If it doesn't, no problem. Use something completely different. Just promise me that when you do, you'll let us know. Post it online and tag #YourNewPlaylist so we can see it too!

Whoa, this chapter got long on us. I like the short ones better because they make me feel like I accomplished something. If you like the short ones too, then you're in luck. I checked with McRae, and the conclusion isn't long. In fact, it's the shortest chapter in this entire book. And it better be where that $20 bill your parents promised you for reading this book is waiting.

Conclusion

I (McRae) never made the lacrosse team again.

Wouldn't it be awesome if I had? Isn't that supposed to be how books like this end? My parents hire a coach from Switzerland who trains me at four o'clock every morning. I start carrying logs on my back while running sprints up hills in the snow. I change to an all-plant diet and put myself on a personal mission to dominate that lacrosse field at next year's tryouts!

Only that's not what happened.

I got cut. I got sad. I got to work on some new soundtracks.

I told myself the truth, things like, "My lacrosse friends won't unfriend me just because I was cut" and "Our high school won the lacrosse state championships last year, so it's a hard team to make."

I asked the three magic questions whenever broken soundtracks got loud again: Is it true? Is it helpful? Is it kind?

I looked at my symbols. (Thanks for the trunk shout-out, L.E.!)

I remembered JEEPS and the five good actions that help me feel better.

I did everything I could to tap into the superpower of mindset instead of letting broken soundtracks run the show.

And a few days later I joined the cross-country team.

That won't be the last challenge I face. I'm only 16 after all. But it won't be the last opportunity I face either, because I'm just getting started. That's my favorite soundtrack from this whole book and the one I want to leave you with right now.

We have our entire lives ahead of us. We have the only thing all the money in the world can never buy: time. And better than that, we have the power and permission to create new playlists that will encourage us every step of the way. I don't know what you'll put on yours, but I know what's at the top of mine:

I'm just getting started!

P.S.

Can books have a P.S.? Or is this more of a bonus chapter and less of a P.S.? We're not sure . . . this is the first book McRae and I have written, so we're kind of in "winging it" territory.

All we know is that there are six things we students need to hear from our parents that are sometimes hard for them to admit. We thought it might be good for our dad to share them because he's an author and that's kind of his job. Here he is, with . . .

6 Things Parents Never Tell You

Hats off to you for making it to the end of this book. The average adult only reads seven minutes a day, so you're already dunking on people a lot older than you. You're very rare, and rare people deserve to know the truth. Here's the truth about six things parents never tell you.

1. We didn't have a perfect plan when we were your age.

Has an adult ever asked you, "What are you going to do next?" Of course they have. That's one of our favorite questions. Other variations include: "What do you want to be when you grow up?" "What are you doing after high school?" and "What's your plan after college?" These questions are fine, but not when they're delivered with a degree of pressure that implies you should have a perfect plan by now.

It's tempting as a student to think that adults who are in their forties knew exactly what they were going to do when they were 22 or 18 or 16, but I have a confession: we didn't. No one did. OK, maybe that one guy who always wanted to be a podiatrist knew he was going to attend podiatry school, study feet, and eventually open his own practice in Carmel, Indiana. That guy knew perfectly, but most of us didn't even like him.

When I was 16, I didn't know what I would be doing at age 46. How could I? Social media, one of the biggest parts of my job, didn't even exist then. I couldn't have majored in social media management when I was in college because TikTok, Twitter, You-Tube, Facebook, and Instagram hadn't been created yet. I couldn't have even told you at age 24 that I would be an author. I didn't write my first book until I was 34.

Pick a great major if you go to college. Find a job that fits your strengths and abilities. Listen to the advice of guidance counselors and teachers about what's next, but don't feel like you have to have it all figured out yet. Any adult who tells you they knew exactly what they were going to do when they were your age is a liar.

2. We (mostly) don't know what we're doing as parents.

The other day someone asked me, "How do you parent in a way that prevents your kid from needing to go to a therapist later?"

I told them, "You don't. Next question."

I know that someday L.E. and McRae are going to tell a counselor about the mistakes I made as their dad. How do I know? Because I keep doing dumb things. Why? Because parenting is hard.

For all you oldest children reading this, you're the first kid we ever had. It's not like you're kid number 36 and we worked out the kinks on the first 35. (By the third kid, though, we've got a bit of a handle on things. For instance, we know you won't die if you eat something off the floor. First kid gets a five-second rule. Third kid gets a five-minute rule.)

Having a kid is one of the wildest experiences in the world. On the day you were born, do you know what happened? A doctor handed you to us and then essentially said, "Good luck with this!" and disappeared. There were half a dozen nurses and doctors in the room, but as soon as they made the handoff, they vanished.

We stood there holding this tiny miracle that doesn't come with a manual. I didn't even know how to get you properly buckled into your car seat, never mind what to do when mean girls gossip behind your back. *Mean Girls* isn't a movie. It's a documentary.

We're figuring it all out on the fly, and sometimes we make mistakes. So will you. You've never been a student before. You've never been a teenager before. And you shouldn't be expected to be an expert either. Let's use two really simple soundtracks that will help us have a little bit of empathy for each other.

The next time I mess up, I'm going to say, "I'm sorry, this is my first time being a parent."

The next time you mess up, you should say, "I'm sorry, this is my first time being a teenager."

It's not an excuse for bad behavior. It's an invitation to having a little bit more grace for each other.

MEAN GIRLS ISN'T A MOVIE.
IT'S A DOCUMENTARY.

3. We would have made the same mistakes you're making with your phone.

One of the silliest things we parents do is JUDGE the way you use your phone.

We tell you to stay off it. We yell that you're spending too much time on it. We fuss about Netflix and Instagram and TikTok and every other app.

Why is this silly? Because at your age we would have made the same mistakes you're making with your phone if we'd had one. But we didn't. It's not that I was a mature senior in high school who was deliberate about his screentime and had good boundaries for social media. I just didn't own a phone because no one did.

If I had a phone, it would have been difficult for me. I can't imagine what that *Alice in Wonderland* collection of temptations would have done to my little head. It would have been a struggle for certain, and I would've been grounded constantly. I would've dropped that phone a billion times too. I would've had one of those shattered screens that cuts your finger every time you use it because it's so jagged. And I would've constantly wrecked my dad's 1987 Mazda 323 because I would have been texting and driving.

I didn't need to worry about any of that, though, because I didn't have a phone.

WE WOULD HAVE MADE THE SAME MISTAKES YOU'RE MAKING.

The same goes for video games. I grew up on Nintendo. It wasn't connected to the internet because that didn't exist. I couldn't play it with a friend unless that friend came to my living room and sat next to me. I couldn't go on long, immersive missions that spanned entire universes that contained more computing power than the first space shuttle. All I could do was try to eventually fight Mike Tyson or use the Contra code (your parents will understand).

One of the things that makes parenting hard is that you're experiencing things we never experienced. I didn't have a global pandemic that shut down my school. I didn't have to try paying attention for eight hours on Zoom. I didn't need to learn algebra from a poorly lit, impossible-to-hear video lesson. You did.

When we parents remember that, it's a whole lot easier to understand where you're coming from. If we sometimes act like we would've handled the phone, the internet, video games, the pandemic, or anything else that's new better than you, please know we're wrong.

We would have made the same mistakes you're making.

4. We get stressed out too.

Has an adult ever told you, "It's not a big deal"? Maybe in the middle of a stressful moment—in an attempt to get you to calm down—that phrase has made a cameo? If it has, allow me to apologize, because it's just not helpful.

Saying "It's not a big deal" never fixes the situation. I've never said that to L.E. or McRae about a big exam, a tryout, or a friend drama and had them say, "Thanks, Dad, that makes everything better." It's also not true. We might know that a history test won't matter when you're 45 years old, but guess what? You're not 45 years old right now. A history test matters a lot when you're 15. It's a legitimate, appropriate cause for concern, and in chapter 10 L.E. explained why that happens at the brain level.

But the reason I really don't like the phrase "It's not a big deal" is that it gives you the impression that we don't stress out over things in our own life. It creates this illusion that maybe we adults don't overthink things, maybe we don't worry, maybe we don't have "big deals" that take up a lot of head space in our own lives. So let me be clear right now: we do.

We get stressed out too.

After you go to bed, we stay up and think about taxes. We wonder if some politician is going to do something stupid that makes our life a little bit more annoying. We replay a conversation we had with our boss yesterday over and over again in our heads. We get frustrated that a coworker isn't carrying their weight on a big project.

You know how you hate that lazy kid who doesn't carry his weight in group projects in high school? Yeah, we work with that kid now—except he's 38 and even lazier.

We have our own big deals too. We have our own stresses. We have our own broken soundtracks. Hopefully, by this point in life, we've learned a few ways to deal with them. Hopefully, despite not having it all figured out, we have figured out a few things. Hopefully, instead of pretending we're perfect when you're feeling stressed, we'll be brave enough to say, "Me too sometimes. Here's what I've found that helps."

That way we get to work on it together side by side, like a team.

Parents get stressed out too. That's just part of being human. But we can both do something about it.

5. We make you do braver things than we do.

Another parent admitted that to me once when I was on a business trip in Phoenix, Arizona, and it knocked me over. She was right.

Have you ever thought about how brave we parents ask you to be?

Think about it: We sign you up for soccer when you're six years old. We say, "Hey, here's a sport you've never played, with people you've never met, coached by someone you don't know. Go on. Run out onto that field full of complete strangers and just see how that goes."

Every year of school you essentially get a brand-new job. You change classes, teachers, subjects, buildings—there's no end to the list of new things you have to do when you're a student.

Meanwhile, if my wife tells me we're going to a dinner party, I ask a thousand questions:

"Who's going to be there?"

"Will I know anyone?"

"Are we riding there with anyone or driving alone?"

"How long are we staying?"

"How far away is it?"

HAVE YOU EVER THOUGHT ABOUT HOW **BRAVE** WE PARENTS ASK YOU TO BE?

JON ACUFF

#YourNewPlaylist

"What kind of food will they have?"

"Do we have to go?"

I'm trying to carefully manicure the evening so that it's not awkward. I'm doing everything I can, all day, to prevent change from causing me any frustration. We adults get stuck in careers, friendships, neighborhoods, and our own drama, all the while asking our teenagers to calmly deal with constant change in their own lives.

We ask you students to be braver than we're being.

It doesn't have to be that way. Adults can be brave too. We can try new things. We can change jobs. We can pick up a new hobby. We can reinvent ourselves. We're works in progress, just like you, but all too often we don't give you enough credit for being the bravest person in the house.

Thanks for setting an example that even we adults can learn from.

6. We're control freaks because we love you.

Speaking of bravery, I was blown away when McRae said she wanted to include her story of getting cut from the lacrosse team in this book. She had worked really hard to make the team, loved being on that

team, wore that lacrosse jacket with so much pride
. . . and then got cut. She dreaded that moment, but
so did her mom and I.

The hardest part of parenting is watching you go
through hard times. Whether it's a team you don't
make, a dance you don't get invited to, a friend
group you get pushed out of, a class you struggle
with, or a million other challenges, we parents hate
to see you wrestle with all the obstacles life throws at
you.

Sometimes, in our desire to protect you, we can
be overbearing. That sounds a little better than "control freaks," but the result is the same. We become
helicopter parents or snowplow parents or whatever
phrase best captures the act of trying to organize
every inch of your life until there's not a single moment of pain.

But it's not good for you. Manicuring your life so
that there aren't any challenges removes your ability
to grow. Fixing all your problems steals the strength
and confidence you'll gain from working on them
yourself.

We know that deep down, but it's still tempting
to sculpt your world in such a tightly controlled
manner that the threat of all discomfort is removed.
In moments like that, it's completely fair for you to
proclaim, "My parents are the worst!" But just know

that usually it's because we're trying to give you the best and just got things a little bit twisted.

We're control freaks sometimes, but it's not because we don't trust you. It's because we know how hard the world can be, and we'd do anything to protect you from that for as long as possible.

There are probably other things I'm forgetting, parenting secrets that really don't need to be secrets any longer, but those are the six I think about the most.

Show this section to your parents. Maybe it will start a conversation. Maybe it will start a connection. Maybe they'll share a story from their own adolescence that you've never heard before.

Even better, maybe they'll give you that $20 bill they owe you for finishing this book!

Acknowledgments

From McRae

First off, I would like to thank the amazing people behind the scenes of this book. Baker Books, thank you so much for this fun opportunity. Thank you, Brian Vos, for teaching me what a great editor does for a book. Thanks to all my friends from church: Jamie Myatt, Kayla Delatorre, Alicia Alexander, and Allie Bales. You guys love me so well. Shout-out to Mrs. Brannon's sixth-period study hall where I wrote a majority of this book. Thank you, Aunt Lori, for being an amazing aunt and for using your expertise to help improve the book. A huge thanks to my dad for working hard with me to turn my dream of writing a book into a reality. I published a book before

I graduated high school! I am still pinching myself! Last but not least, whether you are a student or adult, thanks for reading this book! I hope reading it helps you as much as writing it helped me.

From L.E.

Baker Books, if this is what it's like to publish a book, no wonder my dad loves your team so much! Thanks for guiding me through this process. Brian Vos, thanks for essentially teaching a class on "How to Write Your First Book." Your insight made writing this book really fun! Thank you, Amy Fenton, for being my small group leader so faithfully for so many years. I'm who I am today because of your wisdom and kindness. Thank you, Mr. Campos, Mr. Aydelott, and Ms. V: your leadership with the Franklin Band taught me discipline, teamwork, and the value of hard work. College and the rest of my life will be different because of how you care for students like me. Mom, thanks for encouraging us each step of the way. The "Jenny Edit" always makes Acuff books so much better. Dad, thanks for including us in what just might be the best career on the planet. I loved writing this book with you!

From Jon

A special thank-you to every parent who asked for this book long before it existed. Without your early encouragement, we wouldn't have written it. Thank you to Baker Books for believing in this project. Brian Vos, you don't just help me edit books, you shepherd them. Mark Rice, thanks for always having a creative answer to the question "How do we share this book with the world?" Amy Nemecek, Eileen Hanson, Dwight Baker, and the entire sales team, thanks for being such wonderful partners in this publishing adventure. Mike Salisbury and Curtis Yates, it's hard to believe this is the fourth book we've done together. I can't wait for the next four! Lori Windham, thank you for reading the manuscript and sharing your expertise. Your wisdom proved invaluable. Jenny, your name might not be on the cover, but just like every book I write, you're on every page. L.E. and McRae, high school is challenging enough, and then your dad says, "Let's write a book!" Thank you for your hard work, creative ideas, and willingness to remove all my dad jokes. I love you both!

Notes

Chapter 2 The Wrong Songs

1. Daniel Kahneman, *Thinking, Fast and Slow* (New York: Farrar, Straus and Giroux, 2015), 53–54.

Chapter 7 The Dial and the Switch

1. Quoted in Jon Acuff, *Soundtracks: The Surprising Solution to Overthinking* (Grand Rapids: Baker Books, 2020), 63.
2. Acuff, *Soundtracks*, 63.

Chapter 10 All Your Favorite Songs

1. Jia Jiang, *Rejection Proof: How I Beat Fear and Became Invincible through 100 Days of Rejection* (New York: Harmony Books, 2015), 65.

Chapter 12 There's Great Music Everywhere

1. Stephen Scoggins, "Turn Overthinking into a Super-power: Jon Acuff," *Stuck to Unstoppable* (podcast), episode 50, June 1, 2021, https://stephenscoggins.com/turn-overthinking -into-a-superpower-john-acuff/.

About the Authors

Jon Acuff is the *New York Times* bestselling author of eight books, including *Soundtracks: The Surprising Solution to Overthinking* and the *Wall Street Journal* #1 bestseller *Finish: Give Yourself the Gift of Done*. When he's not writing or recording his popular podcast, *All It Takes Is a Goal*, Acuff can be found on a stage as one of INC's Top 100 Leadership Speakers. He's spoken to hundreds of thousands of people at conferences, colleges, and companies around the world, including FedEx, Range Rover, Microsoft, Nokia, and Comedy Central. Known for his insights wrapped in humor, Acuff's fresh perspective on life has given him the opportunity to write for *Fast Company*, the *Harvard Business Review*, and *Time* magazine. Jon lives outside of Nashville, Tennessee, with his wife, Jenny, and two teenage daughters, the authors, L.E. and McRae. To learn more, visit Acuff.me.

@jonacuff   @authorjonacuff

L.E. Acuff is a freshman business major at Samford University in Birmingham, Alabama. In addition to writing books, she loves skimboarding, Frisbee, and skiing. When she's not behind a laptop, she's creating clothing at her sewing machine or music at her piano.

McRae Acuff is a junior at Franklin High School in Franklin, Tennessee. She runs cross-country and track, loves student government, and is somewhere babysitting right now. She's a writer at heart and will probably write the follow-up to *Your New Playlist* all by herself. She and her dad sincerely hope this book helps her get a college scholarship.

Soundtracks

The Surprising Solution to Overthinking

The *Wall Street Journal* bestselling book that started it all!

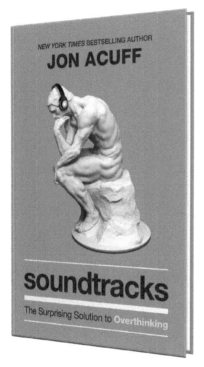

Overthinking isn't a personality trait. It's the sneakiest form of fear.

It steals time, creativity, and goals. It's the most expensive, least productive thing companies invest in without even knowing it. And it's an epidemic.

In *Soundtracks*, *New York Times* bestselling author Jon Acuff offers a proven plan to change overthinking from a super problem into a superpower.

When we don't control our thoughts, our thoughts control us. If our days are full of broken soundtracks, thoughts are our worst enemy, holding us back from the things we really want. But the solution to overthinking isn't to stop thinking. The solution is running our brains with better soundtracks. Once we learn how to choose our soundtracks, thoughts become our best friend, propelling us toward our goals.

If you want to tap into the surprising power of overthinking and give your dreams more time and creativity, learn how to DJ the soundtracks that define you. If you can worry, you can wonder. If you can doubt, you can dominate. If you can spin, you can soar.

Book an Acuff (or two) at your next live event!

Jon is one of INC's Top 100 Leadership Speakers. He's spoken to hundreds of thousands of people at conferences, colleges, and companies such as Nissan, Lockheed Martin, and Nokia. Known for his insights wrapped in humor, Jon always provides a mix of inspiration and instruction that leaves audiences ready to turn their ideas into actions.

L.E. and McRae are no strangers to the stage. They've spoken to crowds from 80 to 8,000 people. Their fresh approach to student life is a great addition to parenting, college, or teen events.

For more information about booking Jon, L.E., or McRae, visit

BookJonAcuff.com

BIG LIVES START WITH BIG THOUGHTS.

Create Yours with the *Soundtracks* Course from Jon Acuff!

Building on the ideas in this book, Jon walks you through six compelling videos full of activities, exercises, and insights that will help you make the most of your time, creativity, and productivity.

LEARN HOW TO

1. Get more done by turning up the music on every important project.

2. Make faster, smarter decisions with the flip of a coin.

3. Accomplish more goals by beating your pocket jury.

4. Improve relationships by picking the right soundtrack for the right person.

5. Create symbols and turn-down techniques that will make new soundtracks stick.

In addition to exclusive content, you'll get a beautiful workbook to guide you each step of the way.

Watch the free trailer at SoundtracksCourse.com!

5 IDEAS TO SHOUT ABOUT!

Every Friday I (Jon) send out an action-packed, often hilarious collection of pure awesome! These are the kind of ideas that if you came to my house for dinner, my wife, Jenny, would end up saying, "Jon, you're shouting about those ideas. Take it down a notch."

THE IDEAS INCLUDE THE FOLLOWING:

1. Book recommendations

2. Songs you haven't heard but will undoubtedly love

3. Links to fresh videos

4. Things I think are funny

5. Tips on the little corners of life I know a little about (writing, speaking, entrepreneurship, parenting, Yanni, etc.)

And a whole lot more.

Don't miss a single issue. Sign up for free today!

Visit Acuff.me/newsletter